TENERIFFE LACE

edited by JULES & KAETHE KLIOT

Teneriffe lace is a needle lace technique requiring a frame or form in addition to an ordinary needle and thread. It is much akin to needleweaving but with the lace characteristics of openwork and the delicacy and patterns recalling the fine tracery of a spider's web.

Worked over a form, radial "warp" threads are first laid down in a regular fashion. This is followed by weaving and knotting a single "weft" thread with a needle through these radiating threads. Patterns are created by the contrast of solid and open areas, by changing the shapes of open areas, and by the interlocking of free-spanning threads.

This book is a republication of portions of four outstanding manuals printed during the early years of the 20th century, when this technique gained its initial popularity. As happened with other needlework techniques, its popularity dwindled soon thereafter, surfacing briefly during the forties, when a simplified method called "Polka Spider Web" became popular. With the revival of handcrafts of all sorts in recent years, teneriffe lace technique and application should be a welcome addition to every needleworker's vocabulary.

Arranged by section in this text, the original titles of the publications which have contributed to this book are as follows:

SECTION 1. Pg. 3: *TENERIFFE LACE DESIGNS AND INSTRUCTIONS*, 1904, Earl & Co.

This section establishes a vocabulary of designs and basic techniques.

SECTION 2. Pg. 46: *TENERIFFE LACE WORK*, no date (about 1910), DMC.

This section offers a brief history of the lace, describes additional working techniques and illustrates a wide range of motifs and edgings.

SECTION 3. Pg. 72: *THE LACE MAKER*, Vol. 1, No. 2, 1903, Sara Hadley.

This section includes a brief history and yet another method for making the lace as well as offering some over-all designs.

SECTION 4. Pg. 77: *THESA HANDARBEITSBUCH*, no date (about 1920), Handarbeitenhaus Hofman (Germany).

Although of German Text, this section illustrates the wide range of intricate shapes and forms, once available for making this lace. The complex patterns and shapes are beautiful as individual motifs as well as elements to be incorporated into apparel or linens.

The teneriffe designs were originally developed from drawn thread embroidery techniques worked within the confinements of a pre-made fabric. The threads were typically white and of the same size as used for the base fabric. Once the designs were freed from a base fabric, unlimited use of color and thread would be possible.

With minor exceptions, text has been reprinted unabridged and reference to threads and tools are as originally mentioned. Most are no longer available except as might be found in an antique store or flea market. While virtually any thread is suitable, it is suggested that the beginner start with a good crochet cotton such as DMC Cordonnet, sizes 30, 40 or 50, available in white and ecru. A long thin needle is recommended, such as a 3 1/2" "doll needle" which permits ease of weaving.

Teneriffe Lace is always worked on a form which was and can be of a variety of configurations ranging from a stuffed firm pillow, a flat disk or a mechanical three-dimensional device. For the working form today, the traditional hard rubber forms of the "Polka Spider Web" can still be found. These permit the making of round and square motifs in fixed sizes. A firm pillow can be fabricated using sand as a filler or forms can be cut out of stiff pattern stock or heavy plastic. The chapters of this book give ample suggestions for making such forms.

A preferred form, developed by this editor, is the molded plastic grid which can be found in most needlework shops or can be purchased in kit form as a "Teneriffe Kit" listed under suppliers. The grids are perforated throughout and can be found in both rectangular and radial patterns which lend themselves to making virtually any design in any size.

As the use of these grids is truly a modern innovation, the following directions are given as a supplement to the other techniques covered in this book.

The molded plastic grids are available in a variety of sizes and shapes. The sizes most suitable for Teneriffe Lace are the 4" round and square and the large 9" round. For working edgings and larger designs, a larger 11" x 14" grid is available. In using the grid as a working form, a temporary outline or anchorage cord is laid down, and the warp thread looped on to it. When work is completed, the outline thread is cut away and discarded, leaving the lace free.

For square or circular motifs, you can follow the hole patterns for laying out the anchorage cord. For irregular shapes, it is suggested that you draw the outline of the design on the grid with a grease pencil. This is easily be done by laying the grid over your design and tracing the outline.

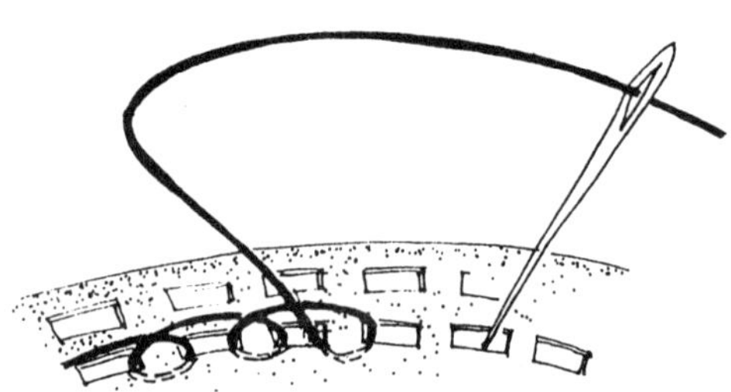

The anchorage cord should be different from the threads used to make your design to avoid confusion when cutting it free. A heavier cord such as crochet cotton of a contrasting color is suggested. The outline cord can be laid down by using either needle or a crochet hook. Using the needle, work around the outline of your design, whipping your cord through the appropriate holes as illustrated. When you reach the starting point, the thread ends can be tied together. If a crochet hook is used, a chain stitch can be worked around your outline, looping through the appropriate holes. This is somewhat faster and permits removal of this cord at the end of the completion of the work without cutting.

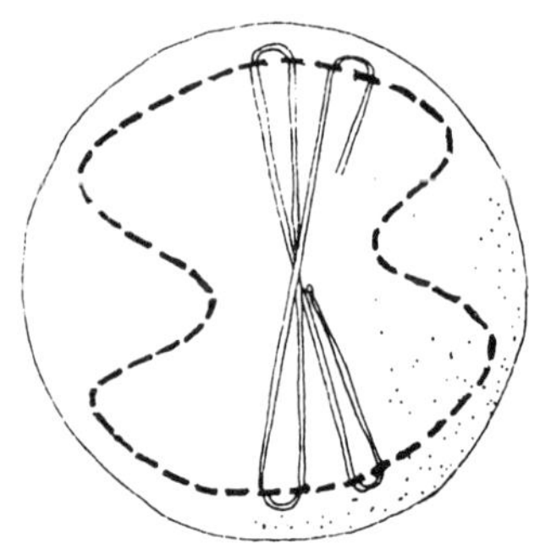

The warping can now proceed. Using about 3 yards of thread and your needle, start at the center of your shape and thread through the bottom of the grid leaving a 4" end underneath. Holding this thread, warp by going under one or two of the loops of the anchorage cord, then crossing the work at the center and then going under one or two of the loops of the anchorage cord on the opposite side. Proceed working back and forth in this manner. All threads should cross at a common center until the shape is completely covered with these radiating threads as the pattern dictates.

Threads should be loose but pulled uniformly as there is considerable take-up as the infilling proceeds. If the grid bends or distorts during warping, you are pulling too tight. When finished with the warping, pull the starting thread end to the top and tie securely around the center crossing with the other free end. Make a square knot and cut the ends short.

The design or weaving process is identical to any of the other Teneriffe methods that will be found throughout this book.

When work is compete, simply tie the free end to the adjacent warp thread. Do not tie to the anchorage cord. Working from the underside of the grid, cut the anchorage cord with fine scissors approximately every inch to free the work.

REFERENCES:

TENERIFFE LACE, Stillwell
ENJOY MAKING TENERIFFE AND OTHER LACE, Kaiser
DMC ENCYCLOPEDIA OF NEEDLEWORK.

SOURCE OF SUPPLY:

LACIS
2982 Adeline St., Berkeley, CA 94703
Teneriffe kits and needles.
For a complete catalog of books, materials and tools for all lace techniques, send $4.00.

LACIS
PUBLICATIONS
3163 Adeline Street, Berkeley, CA 94703

Second Printing, 1994
ISBN: 0-916896-22-6

Teneriffe Lace

THE making of Teneriffe lace wheels, or medallions, is accomplished by several methods; the crude and original way being to arrange a circle of pins on a cushion, using the pin heads to loop the thread upon for the ground work, which is laid like the spokes of a wheel; after which the pattern is woven and knotted.

Different devices have since been invented on which to do the work—some with guides for pins, others with teeth to lace the thread upon, the purpose with all being to simplify the work, making it easy and more interesting.

In working and arranging these designs and instructions, a device has been used having teeth at its edge, each tooth taking the place of the head of a pin. They will, therefore, be referred to as teeth.

A starting point is always indicated, and a point directly opposite or half way round the circle on which the first strands are laid.

Design No. 1

The above illustration is taken from what is probably the best known pattern in Teneriffe lace wheels.

It is a very popular design and will be recognized at once by any one at all familiar with the work, or articles decorated therewith. While attractive and tasteful, it is at the same time a very simple pattern to execute, the skill and knowledge necessary being acquired in a remarkably short time by the merest novice.

The instructions for laying the ground work and making this wheel are in the two following pages. They will give a general idea of how all Teneriffe lace is made, the principal difference being in arranging distances and laying out the pattern, a mere change in the number of threads taken up in knotting often imparting a distinctive character.

Instructions for laying the ground work and working Design No. I

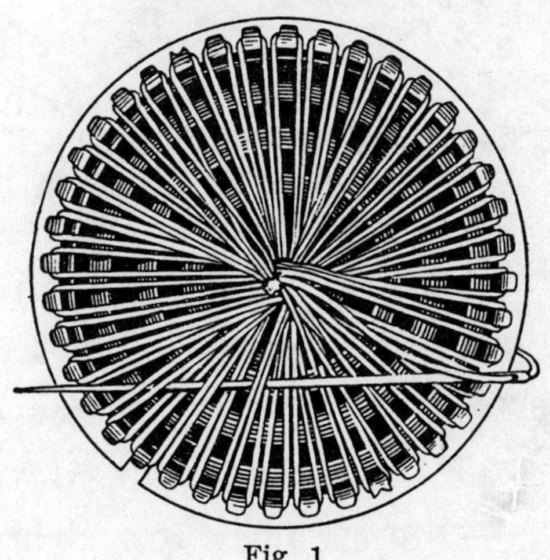

Fig. 1

Lay the foundation thread as follows, and in doing so be careful in starting not to overlap a thread already laid with one following. If jumbled up, it greatly impedes the work, but if care is taken to carry each thread in its own space, the working of the pattern is very easily accomplished.

First make the thread fast either by pinning or in the manner provided by the device you are using. Carry the thread across the circle passing to the right of marked tooth or pin toward you and loop it round the marked tooth directly opposite which is half way round the circle, loop it from left to right, return to marked tooth toward you and loop it from right to left, cross again to tooth at right of marked tooth, loop as at first and return, continue until all the teeth are looped. Break the thread leaving about three feet, thread a needle with this and knot both ends firmly in centre—it will then appear as shown in Figure I.

Should a circle of pins be used on a cushion, take an even number, using black headed ones to mark the half-way stations, a number which is a multiple of four being preferable on which to work the wheel.

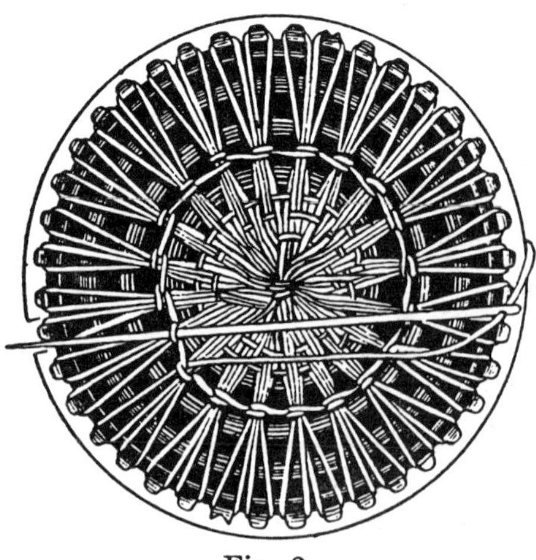

Fig. 2.

The foundation being ready for weaving and knotting, darn three times around the centre, darning the first row rather firmly, taking up two threads at a time as shown in Figure I. In order to alternate the rows of darning, take up four threads instead of two at the beginning of each new row, then continue to take up two at a time; having finished third row of darning, fasten the beginning thread in the centre and then pass the needle through to opposite side to make the darning firm before commencing to knot. The darning of the centre is the first process in working all patterns.

For the first circle of knotting bring the thread a short distance from the darning as shown in Design 1, take four threads, two from each tooth, and finish row as shown in Figure II, draw thread through first knot and pass to next circle of knotting, take four threads, two from the last lot and two from the next to form a cross as in Figure III. For third and last row, take two threads, one from each tooth, knot as close to edge as possible, Figure III.

The side toward you while working is the back of the wheel and shows all imperfections which will not appear when wheel is reversed.

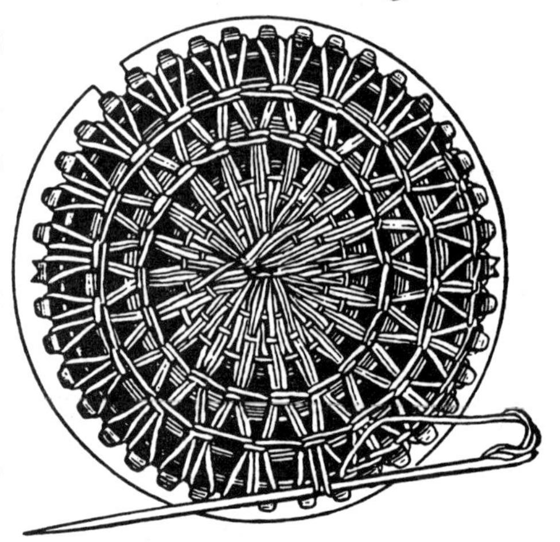

Fig. 3

The Knot

To make the knot, cast the thread in a loop across the threads laid for the groundwork of the wheel as shown in the illustration. Hold the edge of the loop down with the thumb of the left hand, insert needle beyond the far edge of the loop to the right of threads to be knotted, count off the number required according to the design being worked and bring the needle out through the loop. Draw the thread taut and slightly toward the last knot made. It is found preferable to work on the side of the wheel toward, rather than on the far side, always keeping it turned in this position.

Design No. 2

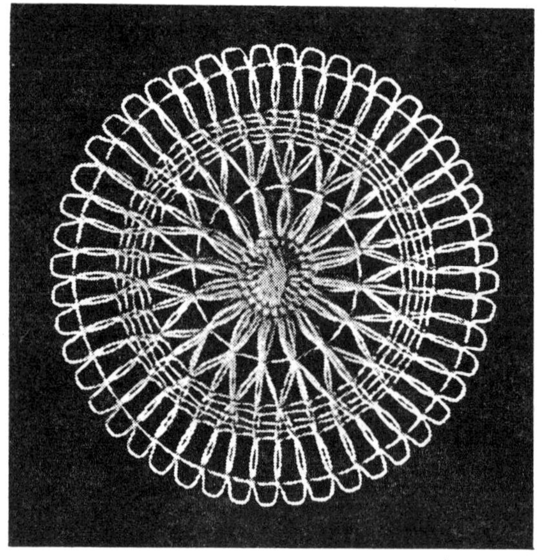

A slight variation is here shown of simply knotting the wheels, three rows of loose weaving having been added to the second row of knots and a row of knotting outside to hold them in place. The design is finished by a row of knotting near the edge. It is easily copied by observing the number of threads taken up for each knot.

Design No. 3

By these small blocks of weaving an otherwise simple design is transformed into one having the firmness of the more solid patterns and still retaining a lace like delicacy in appearance.

Make two rows of knotting before commencing to weave the blocks. In finishing a block carry the thread to line of knotting and fasten, sew the thread around connecting thread and commence the next block. Finish wheel with row of knotting near the edge.

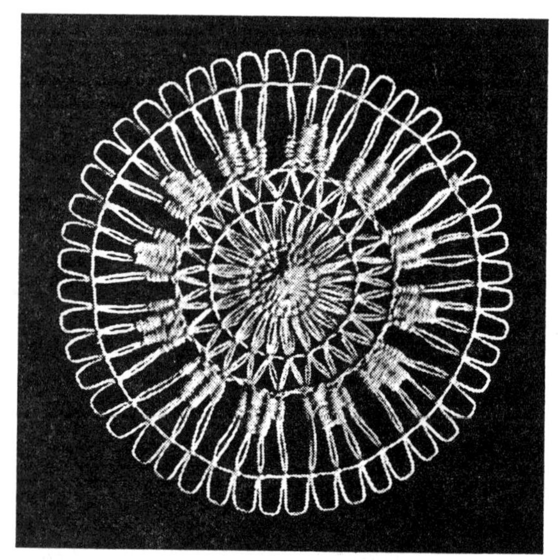

Design No. 4

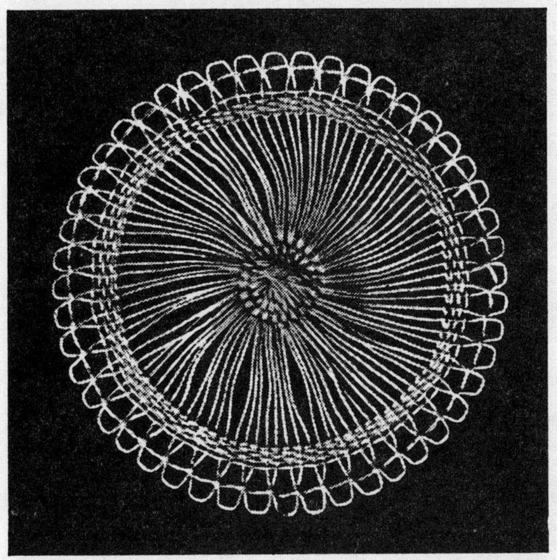

A beautiful lace effect is here obtained which is enhanced when a number of these wheels are used together. Care should be taken to darn the centre into an even circle, a row of knotting is then made a short distance from the outer part of wheel, each thread being knotted separately; to this is added six rows of weaving. Finish design by knotting outer row.

Design No. 5

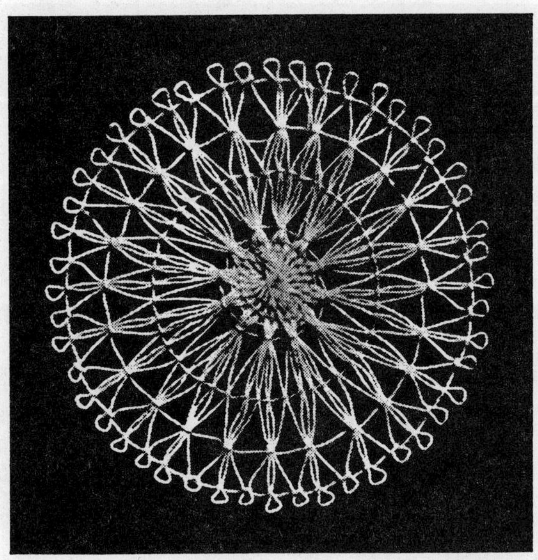

It will be noticed in design No. 5 that the outer edge of loops is varied from those preceding it. In this instance the two threads knotted for the finishing row are taken from one tooth. The first row of knots is commenced as near as possible to the darning in centre.

Design No. 6

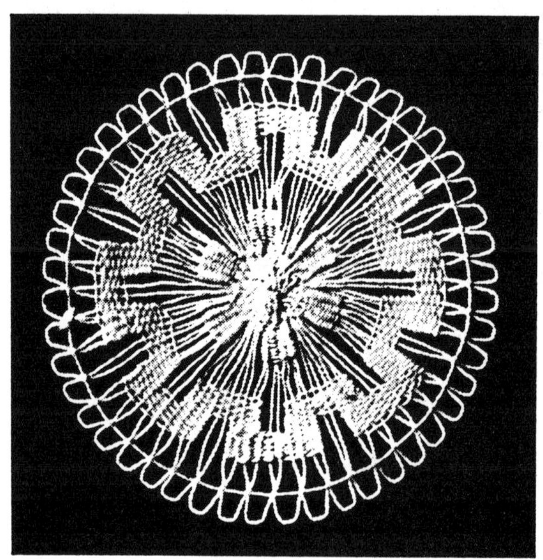

The Grecian Border. After darning centre, weave the short sections, taking two threads at a time. The border is woven one thread at a time, ten strands being woven for the tops of squares and two omitted for each recess. This is in a wheel made of 96 strands. In a wheel made of 80 strands, twelve should be taken for the length of square and four omitted in each recess.

Design No. 7

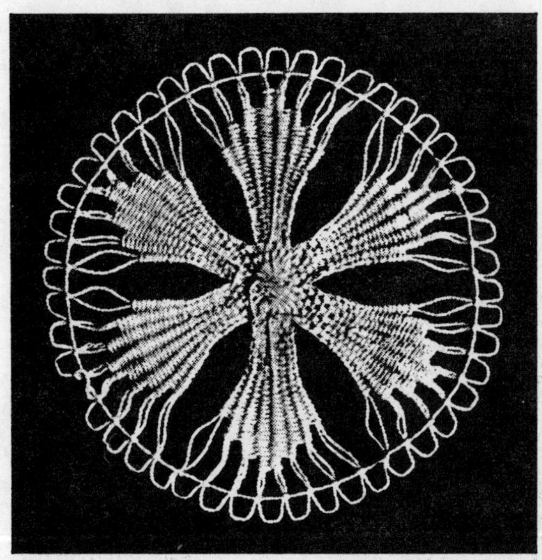

One of the most popular designs in solid weaving is here shown—it may be varied by changing the number of sections, thus making the arms either broader or narrower, but always see before starting to weave that the threads are divisible by the number of arms or sections contemplated.

Darn the centre three times around, then count off the number of threads for each division or section, weave section, taking two threads over and two under, continue until desired length is woven before dropping two threads on either side. For shaping the end, continue a short distance and drop two more on either side; this is repeated until block is finished, return to centre and fasten thread before commencing next block.

Design No. 8

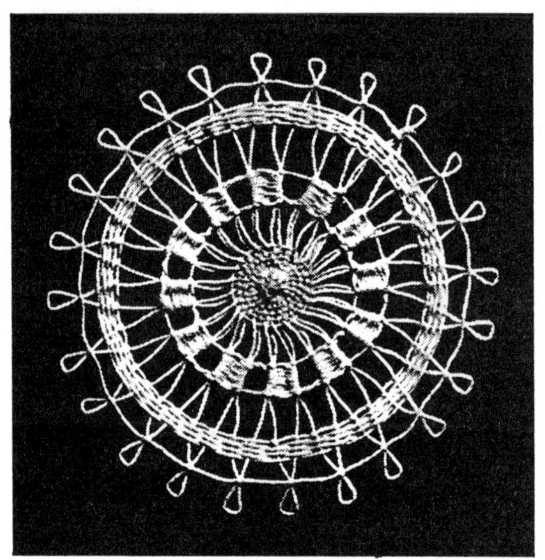

The Pilot Wheel. Use only half the number of teeth laced in the preceding patterns, skipping alternate teeth in laying the ground. After darning, make two circles of knots, two threads to a knot, then weave the small blocks over four threads carrying the thread along the line of knotting in passing from one block to the other. Carry thread out for a circle of weaving, knot each thread of the first or inner row and add six rows of weaving. Finish with a row of knots near the edge, taking both threads from one tooth.

Design No. 9

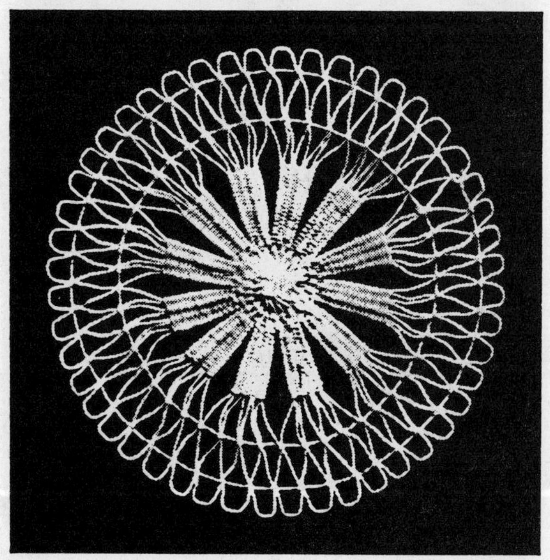

In making this design the threads are divided into equal parts after the centre is darned, the number allowing the division of eight to a section.

In making a wheel with fewer threads see that the sections divide equally. Should the wheel contain eighty threads it would be best to divide it into ten parts, having eight to a part, each tooth counting for two threads.

Weave each section back and forth, two threads at a time, until about half way from the centre, carry thread back to centre and fasten, continue with next section. Finish with two rows of knots as shown.

Design No. 10

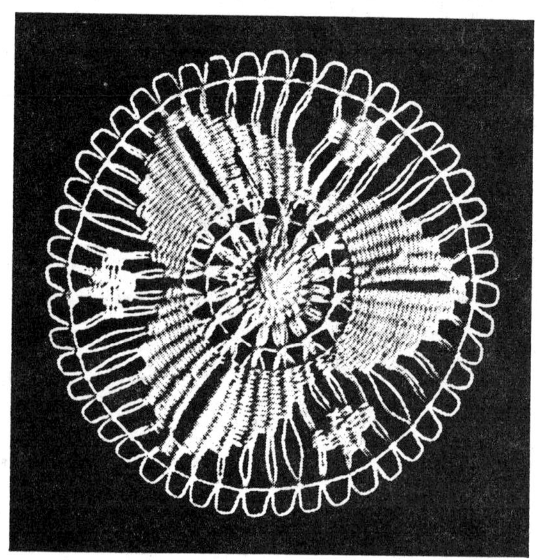

The above design of Egyptian effect is done on a ground whose threads allow of a division into three equal parts. Should a different number be used, it might be necessary to change the number of sections.

A row of knotting is made near the darning; in this instance six threads being taken to a knot. The thread is then carried out as far again as the knots from the last row of darning and a circle of two thread knotting is made; after which the arched wings are woven, care being taken to drop off the outer rows at regular intervals. Always weave from the centre out and finish with a knot. The small blocks are begun and finished with a knot.

Design No. 11

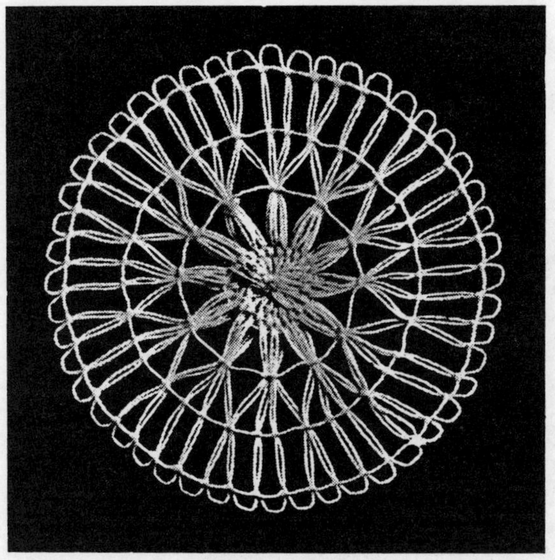

There is but slight difference in the method of working this design from that of Number One, the variation being in the number of threads taken up in knotting. In the first row from darning, eight are taken, in the next row four, then two, twice in succession. The last or outer row has two threads, one from each tooth.

Design No. 12

It will be noticed that Design No. 12 is very similar to Design No. 10, the difference being, that the wings are all inclined in the same direction instead of being grouped in pairs. It must be apportioned according to the number of threads in the wheel. In this instance they are divisible by six and that number has been deemed the most effective. Should the wheel contain eighty threads five or eight divisions are possible, five giving the best results.

Design No. 13

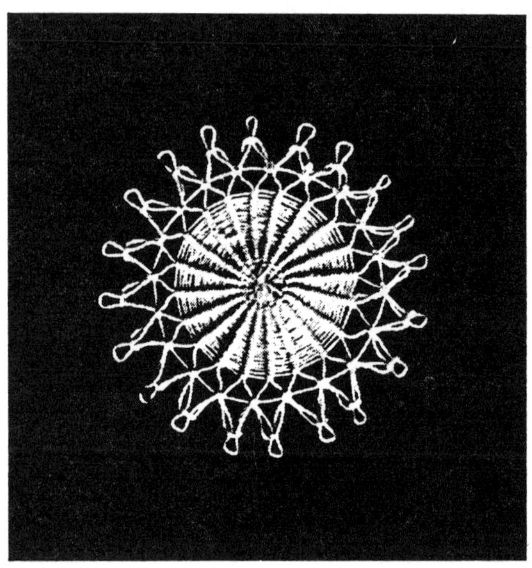

This design is made on a device having forty teeth, only half of them having been used. Begin by lacing every other tooth, and after darning centre, two threads are taken up at a time, the weaving being carried entirely around them and carried to the next two ; this is continued until the solid centre has reached the desired proportions. Fasten thread and make a circle of knotting, carry thread out to loop the ends, and between each loop carry it back to and through the intervening knot. This design is very effective made in closely twisted silk.

Design No. 14

In design No. 14 the effect is shown of making four rows of knotting after darning.

The first row of four threads is made about half way from the centre, the next is of four threads, two from each lot, and the next two rows are made with only two threads to a knot.

Design No. 15

In design No. 15, darn the centre three times around, carry the thread out a short distance, make one row of knots and weave three rows. Separate threads into equal sections and weave the arches four threads to a step, drop two and take up two at completion of each step. On reaching the top step of arch return to centre and weave the other side out to connect with it. Fill in with small blocks, and finish wheel with row of knotting.

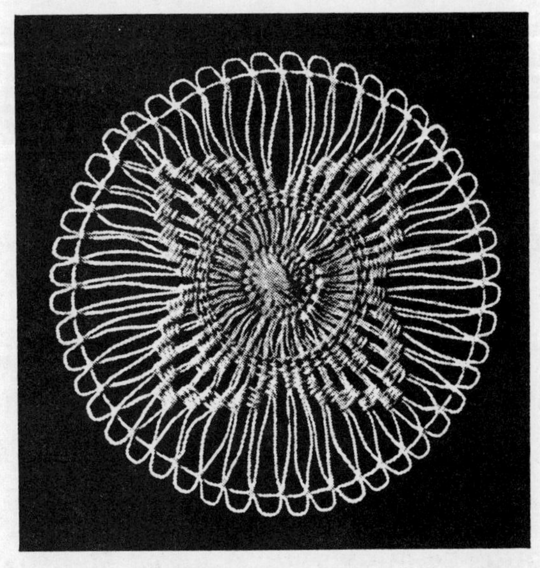

Design No. 16

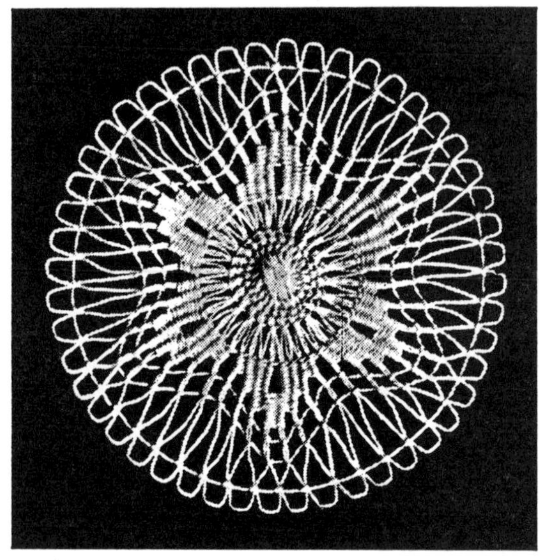

The star in the centre of this design may be made with various numbers of points, but first see that the threads are divisible by the number you wish to make. Darn centre three times and finish with row of knots, eight threads to a knot; move the thread out a short distance and make a row of knots, two threads to a knot as a starting point for weaving. Weave one side of point to height of opening in centre, dropping off two threads on the outside at proper intervals; return and weave other side to same height, then straight across until point is complete. The delicate tracery of knotting surrounding the star may be accomplished with a little care in observing that the points in each section are the same distance from centre as these in the other sections. Some devices are provided with guides for measuring distances, but if the work is done on a pin cushion, it would be advisable to mark the distances off.

Design No. 17

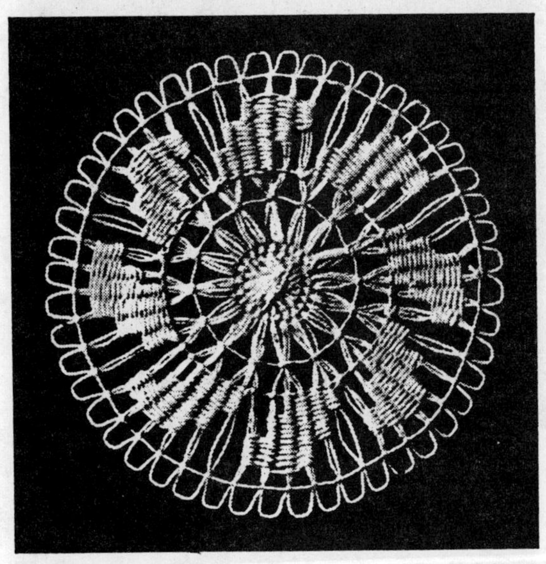

The ninety-six threads here allow of six threads being taken to a knot in the first row. It is just as effective if eight are taken, and sometimes only four are used according to the number of strands in the wheel. The second row is made with but two threads to a knot. Count the threads off into equal spaces and weave the blocks, taking two threads at a time; after weaving several rows to desired height, drop two threads from one side and add two to other; continue a duplicate number of rows and repeat; carry thread back to knotting for next block, passing it through the knot where weaving commences.

Design No. 18

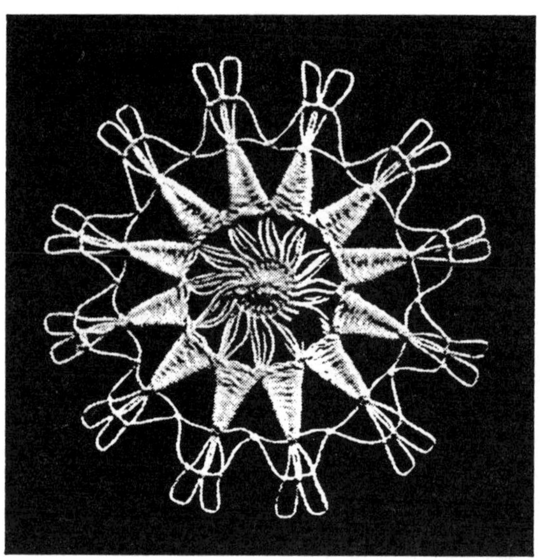

Design No. 18 is an innovation in Teneriffe lace making. The idea is a broader development of what is suggested in Design No. 13. It is entirely new and shows how extensive a field is open to any one having originality in ideas and taste for needlework. It also opens up suggestions for the use of the work in applied garnishes and trimmings not attempted heretofore in home work. Rich effects are obtained by using closely twisted silks, and ornaments for gowns may be made of fine wool, the ground sometimes being laid in silk of the same color—at other times the knotting being silk.

Lay the ground by lacing two teeth and dropping two alternately; darn centre and make two rows of knotting—the first, one-third of the distance from centre, taking four threads; the second, about two-thirds from centre, taking two threads from each lot. Fill in the points of star thus made with weaving. Finish by looping edges with row of knotting, carrying thread back to last row and making fast between each pair of loops.

Design No. 19

Weave three times around centre; then divide threads into four sections and continue weaving over the middle threads of each section. In this wheel, eighteen threads have been woven; weave nearly half way to edge and drop an equal number of threads from each side, and continue weaving, return to centre and repeat in next section; when four are completed, carry the thread to outer edge and make the outside row of knotting, on completion of which, make two straight rows of knotting to points one quarter of the circumference of circle, forming a square; fill in between with two rows of weaving. Finish the design by weaving in the detached blocks.

Design No. 20

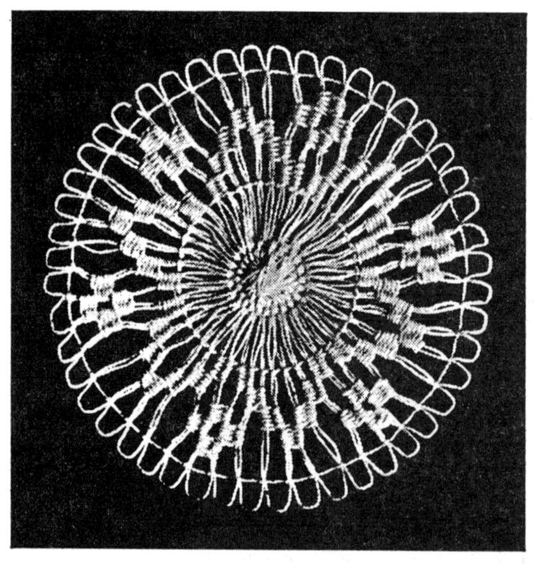

After darning centre, carry thread out and make a row of knotting, taking two threads to each knot; divide threads into equal sections according to number of arches desired, weave arches as in Design No. 16, carry thread to outer edge and make row of knotting, taking one thread from each tooth. Finish with small blocks of weaving between arches.

Design No. 21

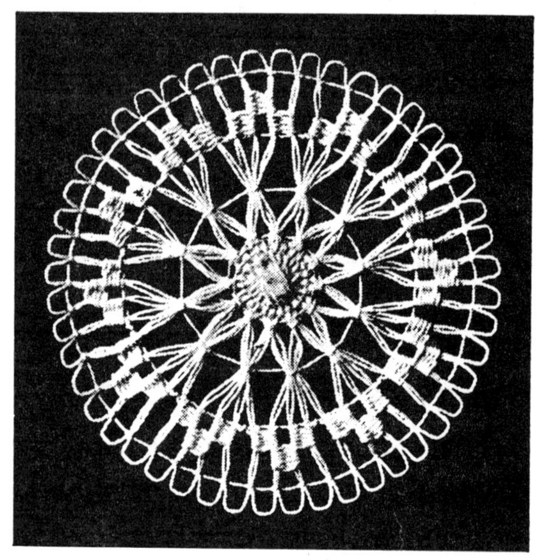

Darn three rows in centre and knot one row, taking eight threads to a knot, carry thread to next row of knotting, taking four threads from each lot, carry thread to third row, taking two threads to each knot. Weave in the small blocks, first seeing that your threads divide properly; if more or less threads are used, it may be necessary to vary the number of threads woven. Finish with row of knotting near the edge.

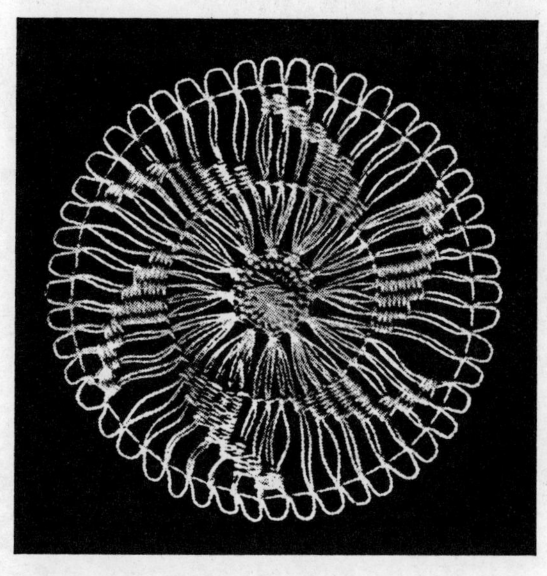

Design No. 22

In Design No. 22 add a row of knots to the darning in the centre, taking eight threads to a knot; carry the thread out to second row and take two threads to each knot, then divide threads into equal sections.

In a wheel of ninety-six threads, divide into six sections ; in a wheel of eighty threads, into five. Weave back and forth over ten threads of section four times, drop the two outer threads and continue four more times, repeat until last four threads have been woven four times, then drop two and add two for each four times until next division of threads is reached. Return to row of knotting and repeat in next section. Finish wheel with row of knotting round the edge.

Design No. 23

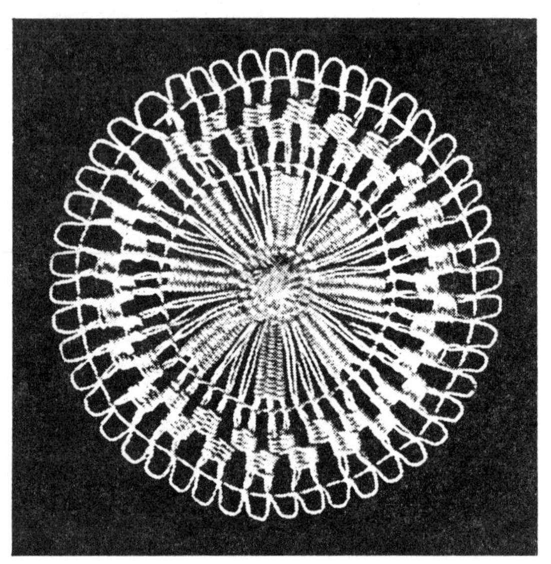

Weave the centre three times and divide thread into equal sections; continue weaving over middle threads of first section half way to outer edge, return to centre, fasten thread and repeat; when all sections are woven, make a row of knotting close to weaving. Next weave the checkered border and finish wheel with outside row of knotting.

Design No. 24

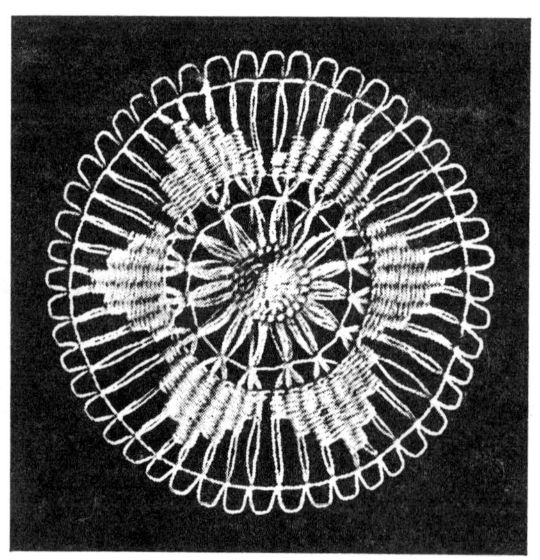

Darn centre and carry thread out, knotting a row of six or eight threads to a knot. Carry thread to next row, knotting two threads to a knot; divide the threads into sections and weave, care being taken to drop outer threads at regular intervals. Finish with row of knotting outside.

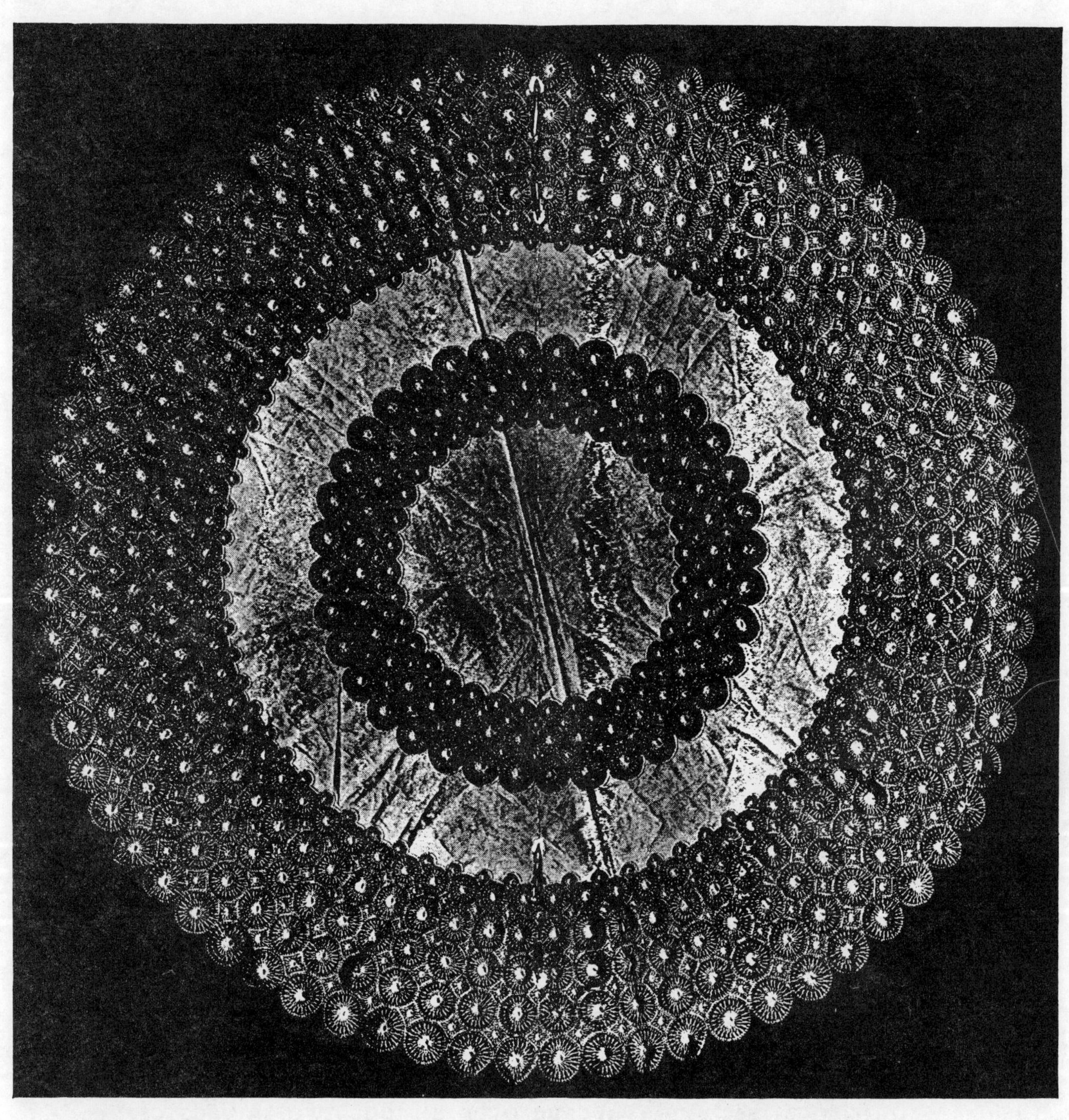

Luncheon cloth made of linen and ornamented entirely with Teneriffe lace wheels.

Design No. 25

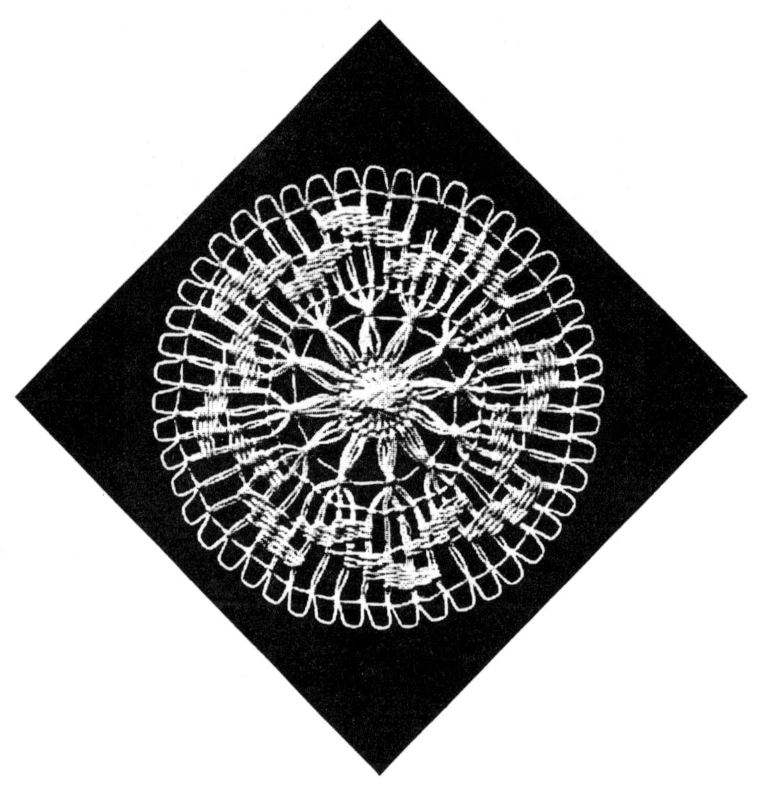

After darning the centre, carry the thread out a short distance and make a row of knots, taking eight threads for each knot. Then carry the thread to the next row of knottings, taking two threads to a knot. The flake-like blocks of weaving are added after dividing the threads into equal sections. Weave over all but two threads of each section—after the inner row is thus made, the outer one is easily added.

Finish wheel with row of knotting near the edge.

Design No. 26

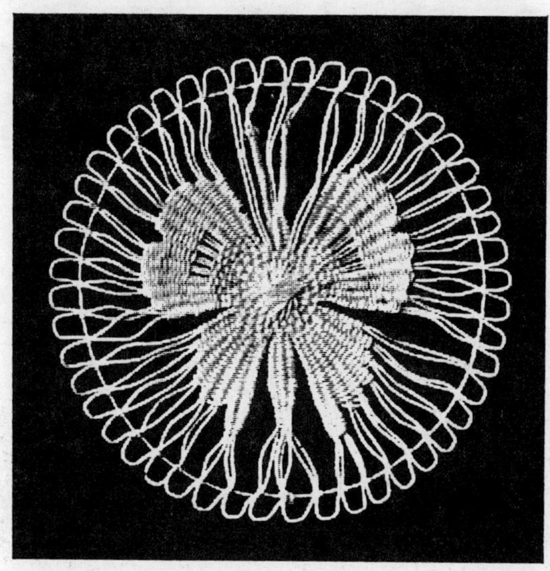

The Butterfly

In making this design the chief point to be observed is laying out the threads in proper proportions.

Darn three times around the centre and then six threads, ten times to make the head, drawing the last few rows rather tight; for the feelers, sew over and over two threads, leaving two threads in between and two on each side of the head.

The large wings are made by weaving twenty-four threads four times, then dropping the eight middle ones and weaving the eight each side ten times, then across the whole twenty-four seven times; drop two threads at each side and weave two rows; drop two more on each side and weave four rows, dividing them in centre to shape wing.

For the lower wings weave sixteen threads eight times, drop outer two and weave twice; repeat until four threads are left, weave these ten times, drawing last rows tight.

Weave body last over six threads twenty times. Finish with row of knotting near edge.

Design No. 27

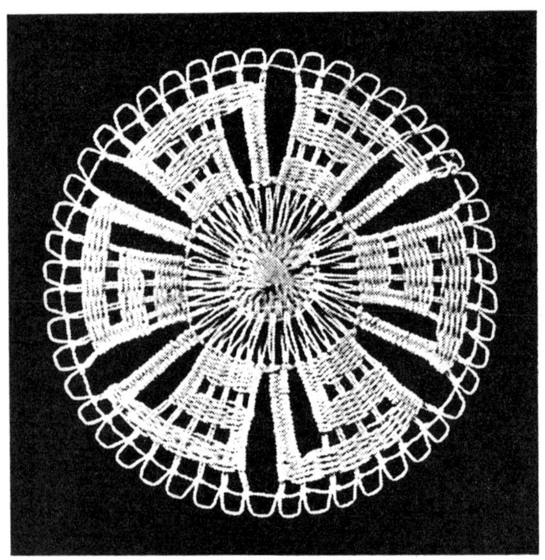

Walls of Troy

The making of this pattern is best accomplished by using care in weaving, pushing the rows together with needle during the progress of the work, and in making the same number of rows in corresponding parts of the different sections.

Commence the wheel by darning the centre; move the thread out the distance shown and make a row of knotting, taking two threads to a knot. Divide the threads into six equal sections and weave back and forth over four threads about forty times, counting for each direction; return to knotting and weave the next twelve threads eleven times; drop the outer eight threads and weave balance nine times, then the twelve eleven times, then the outer four nine times, then over all of the section nine times. These numbers are for a wheel of ninety-six threads.

Finish design with a row of knotting.

Design No. 28

Is made with eighty threads and is about one and one-half inches in diameter.

Darn the centre first three times: divide threads into equal sections, weave four outside threads of each section about six times, then weave straight across five times, drop two threads on each side and repeat. Finish wheel with row of knotting.

Design No. 29

In this design seven rows of knotting have been made, but two threads having been taken to each knot. Always take one thread from each two of the preceding row.

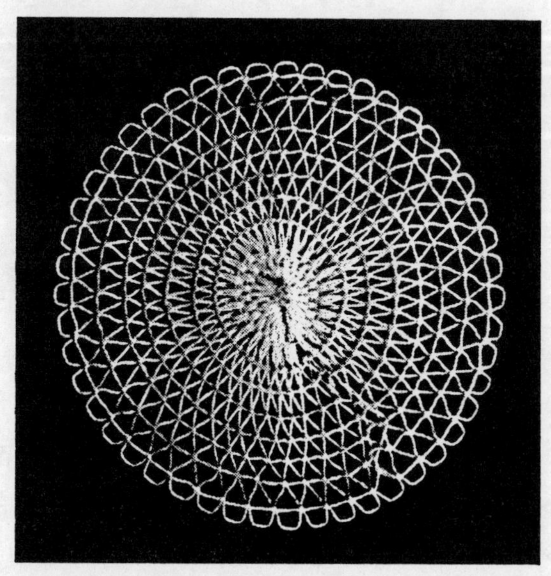

Design No. 30

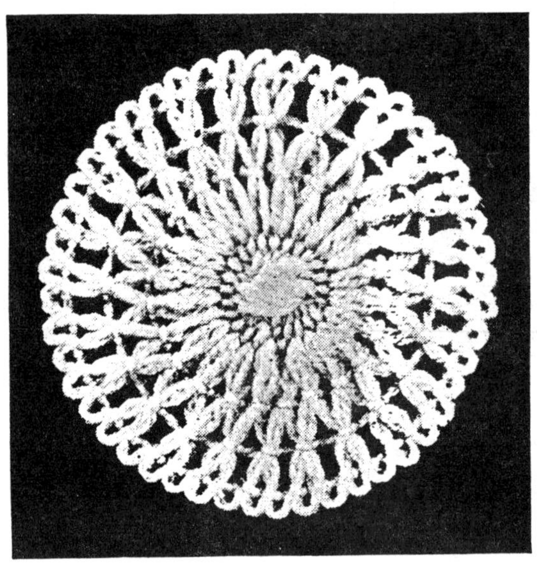

This wheel is made of Saxony wool throughout. Darn centre three times, move to first row of knots, taking four strands to a knot; move to second row, taking two strands from each lot; move to outer row, taking two strands to a knot.

Design No. 31

This design is made of Saxony wool and worked on twenty-four pins or teeth, alternate ones having been skipped in lacing; the centre is first darned, then the weaving is accomplished by carrying the thread entirely around four strands and proceeding to the next four. Repeat this until desired diameter is woven; make a row of knotting two strands to a knot, taking two from the middle for one knot and one from the outside of two lots for the alternate.

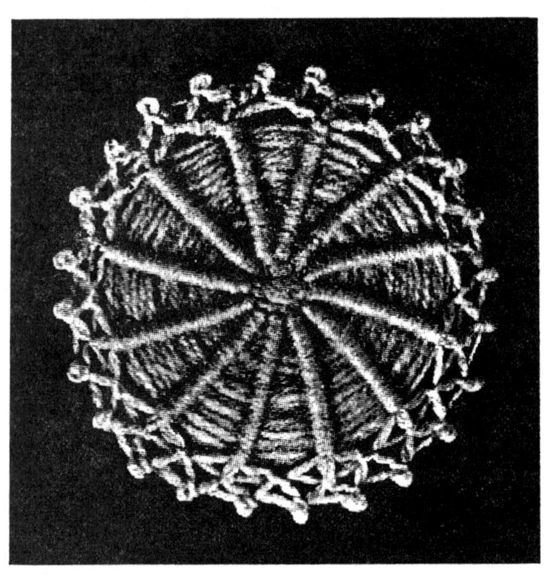

Finish with a row of knotting, taking both threads from the one tooth.

Design No. 32

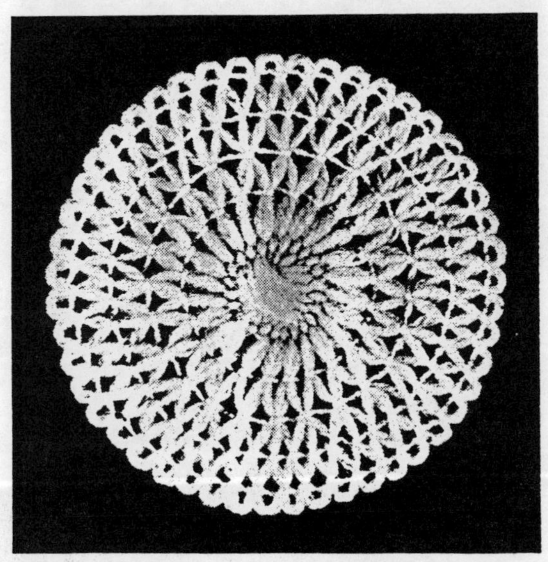

This is a very effective combination of Saxony wool and silk of the same color, the ground being made of wool and the weaving and knotting of tightly twisted silk. This order may be reversed and also the using of matched colors varied, contrasting tints sometimes being adopted as well as the more quiet contrasts of gray and white, etc.

Darn the centre, move to first row of knotting, taking four strands to a knot; for the second row take four, two from each lot; for the third row take two, in one knot, two from the middle, in the alternate, one from each lot. For the outside row take two threads, one from each tooth.

Design No. 33

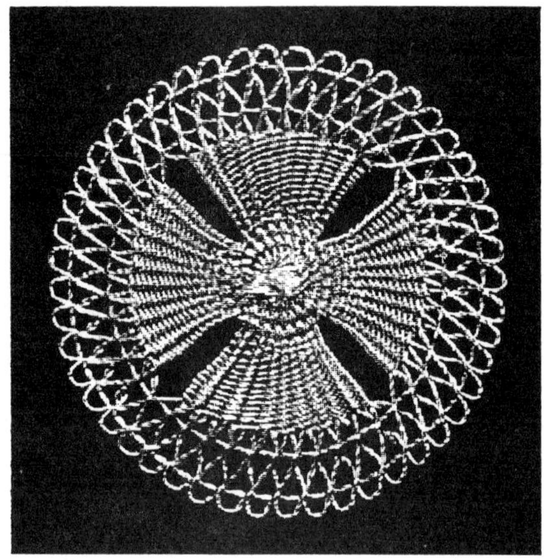

This design is worked with E. E. Embroidery Silk, the solid design in the form of a Maltese Cross having a very rich appearance when worked in this material.

The centre is darned three times, then the threads having been divided into four equal sections; the solid weaving is accomplished by taking two threads under and two over, the length of the section; continue this back and forth until the desired height of arm is woven, return to centre and repeat in the other sections.

Surround the cross with a row of knotting, two threads to a knot, then carry thread out for finishing row.

Design No. 34

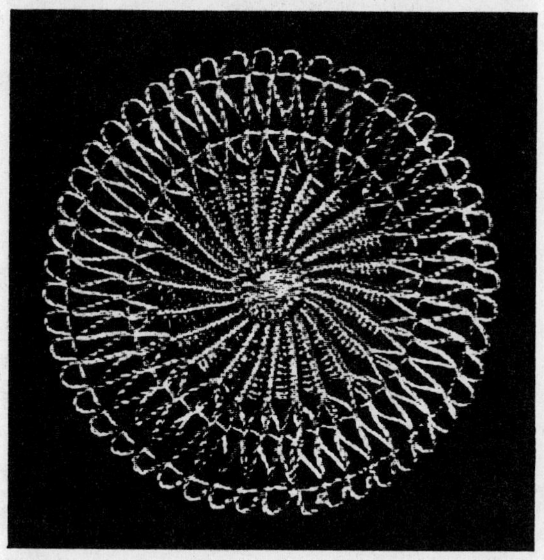

Another design is here shown worked with E. E. Embroidery Silk, the illustration not doing justice to the beautiful effect and lustre of the fabric.

The centre is darned but twice, then a solid block of weaving is accomplished by carrying thread entirely around four strands and proceeding to the next four, continuing this until the desired diameter is reached.

The thread is then carried out for a row of knotting, two threads to a knot, one knot being made from the two centre threads of each group, the alternate from the outside threads of two adjoining groups.

Finish design with a row of knotting near the edge.

Design No. 35

This design is a more open or lacelike pattern in silk and like the two preceding designs it is worked with E. E. Embroidery Silk.

The centre is first darned three times, then the thread is carried out a short distance and a row of knotting is made of two threads to a knot, to this is added four rows of rather open two strand weaving, which is finished with another row of knotting, two threads to a knot.

The thread is then carried out for a row of knotting of four threads to a knot, and the wheel is finished with a row of knotting having two threads, one being taken from each tooth.

Design No 36.

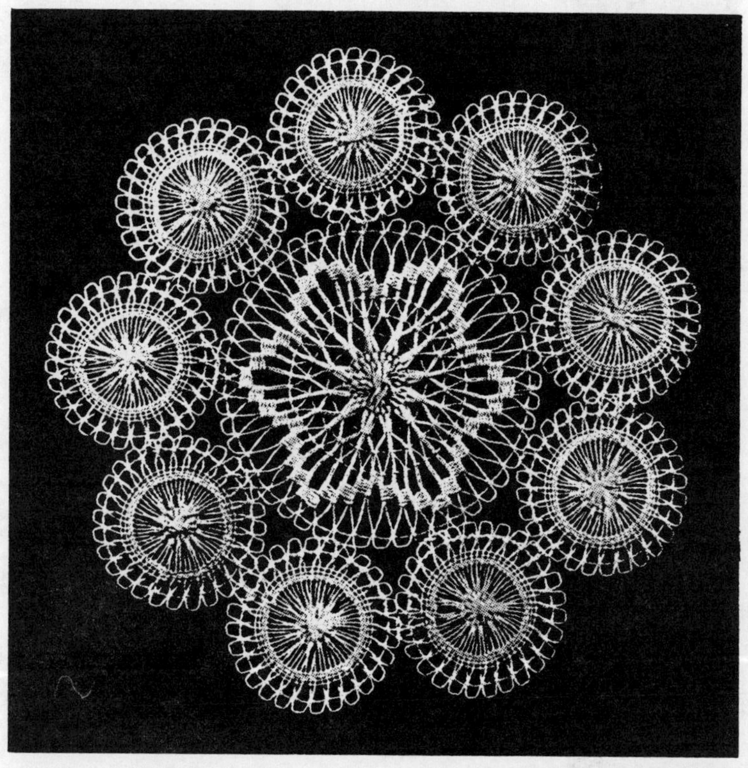

A dainty combination is here shown of the wheels described in Design No. 4, but made with fifty-six threads and about one inch in diameter. They are attached to a wheel two inches in diameter, which is made by first darning the centre, then making a row of knotting, eight threads to a knot; the next row has four threads to a knot, one knot taking two threads from each group, the alternate one, four from the centre. The third row of knotting has two threads to a knot, one knot taking one thread from each group, the alternate taking the two centre threads. The arches are made as in Design No. 15. Finish with row of knotting near the edge.

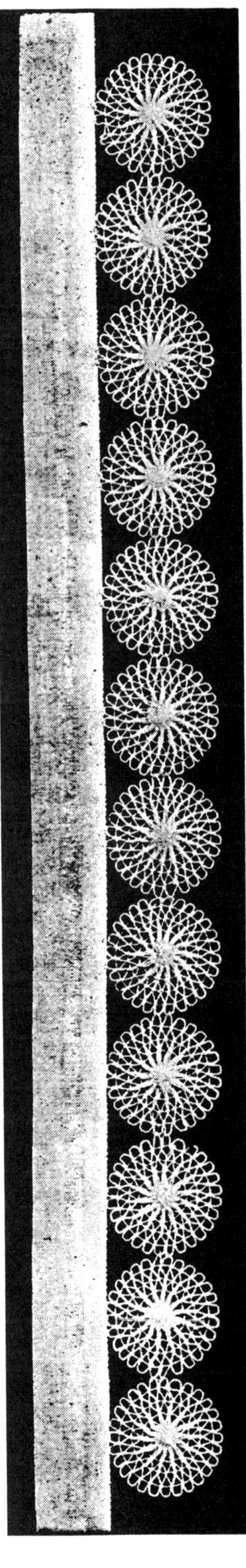

Design No. 37

Stock Collar

The stock collar here shown is made of twelve wheels about one inch in diameter, joined together and attached to a band about half an inch wide which is intended to be turned inside the collar of dress. The wheels have two rows of darning and three of knotting. The first row is of four threads, the second row is of two threads, one knot being made of two threads from the centre of each lot, the alternate of the two outside threads of adjoining lots.

The last row has two threads to a knot, each from a different tooth.

Design No. 38

The doily here shown is made of linen, the wheels are the pattern described in Design No. 1, but any design desired may be substituted.

The wheels are attached to the linen with button-hole stitch, and after they are all in place the linen is cut away. Covers, scarfs, and all manner of table decorations of any size or shape may be made in this manner.

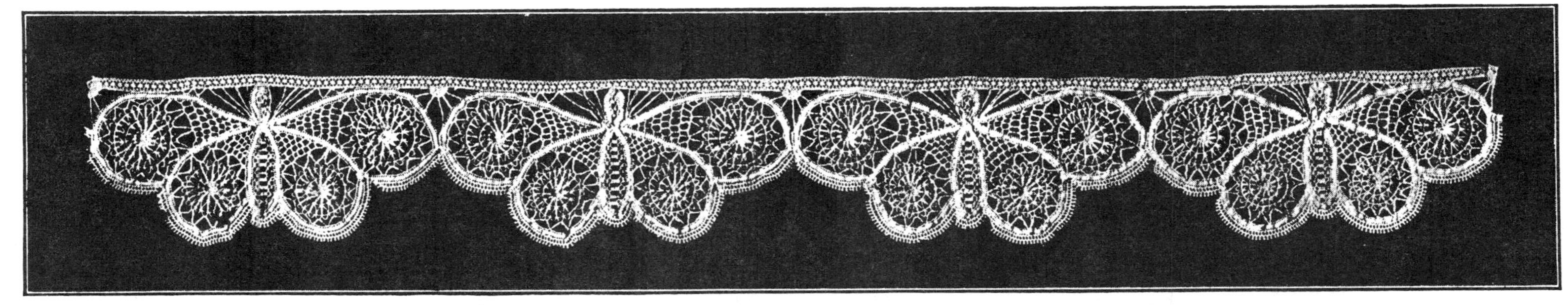

Design No. 39—Bruges Lace

Illustrations of Bruges lace and Bruges insertion of similar design, made of braid and utilizing Teneriffe lace wheels to fill in the ground work, the balance of the pattern being done with stitches.

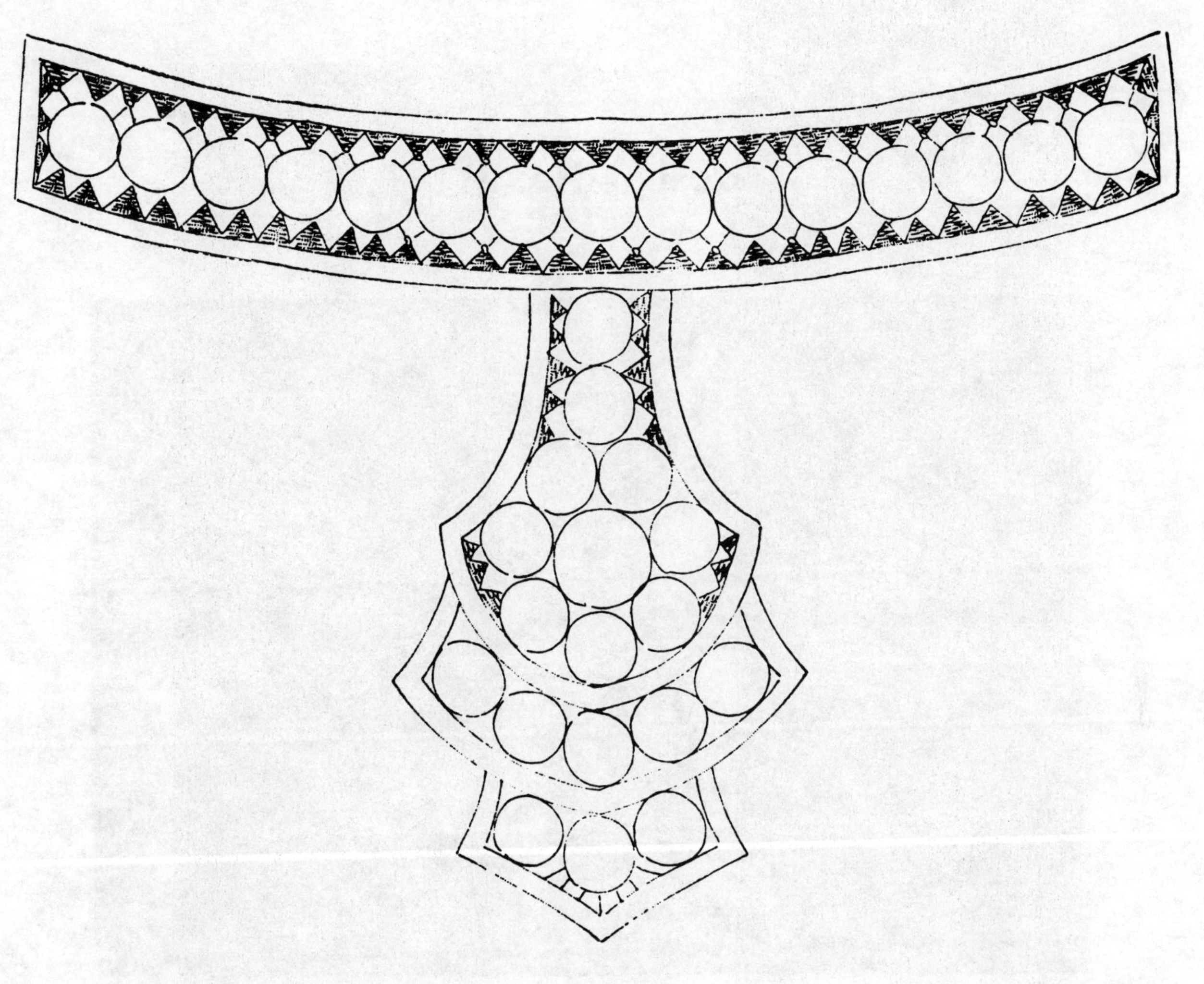

Design No. 40

A large variety of designs and patterns are printed on blue muslin and may be purchased anywhere that fancy work supplies are sold.

They are outlined for the use of braid and lace wheels in combination, the general design of the article is there, but the design for the lace wheel is left to your own taste and pleasure. The accompanying illustration is a sample pattern, and is intended merely as a suggestion.

Design No. 41

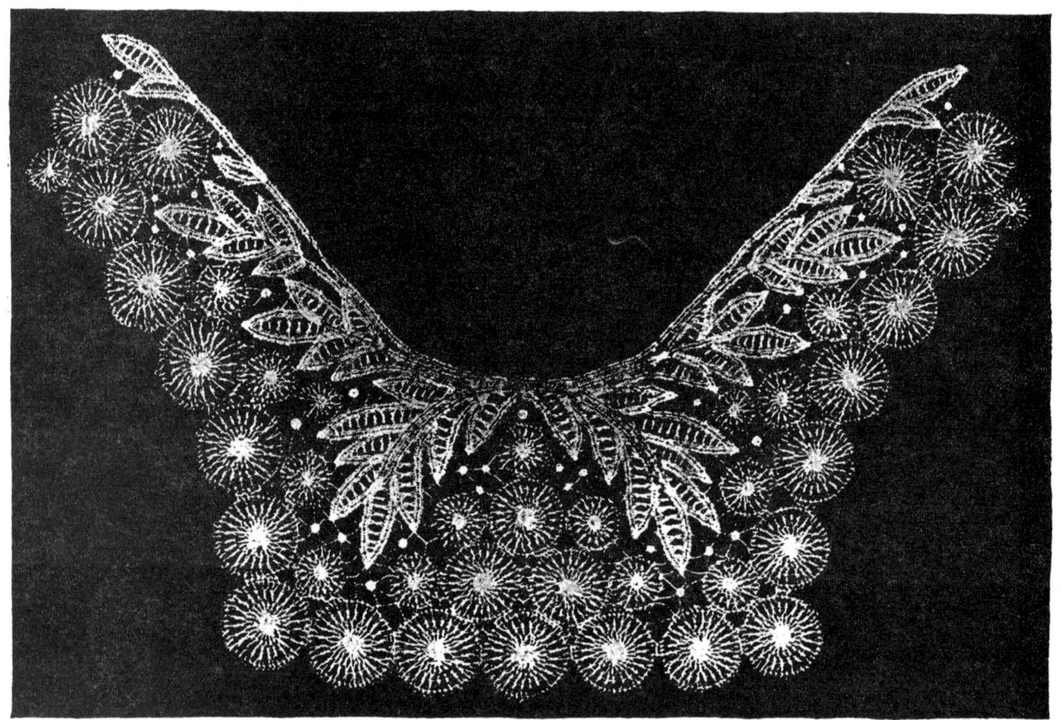

Sailor Collar

This design illustrates the manner of combining Teneriffe wheels with braid to make a sailor collar.

It is advisable to use linen thread in making the wheels for an article of this description and a cambric pattern will be of great assistance in accomplishing the work. In selecting the design for the wheels to be used choose one of the open effects as they will harmonize better with the stitches used in filling in the irregular spaces.

Design No. 42

An effective use is here shown of lace wheels in combination with braid, the irregular spaces being filled in with stitching.

Design No. 43

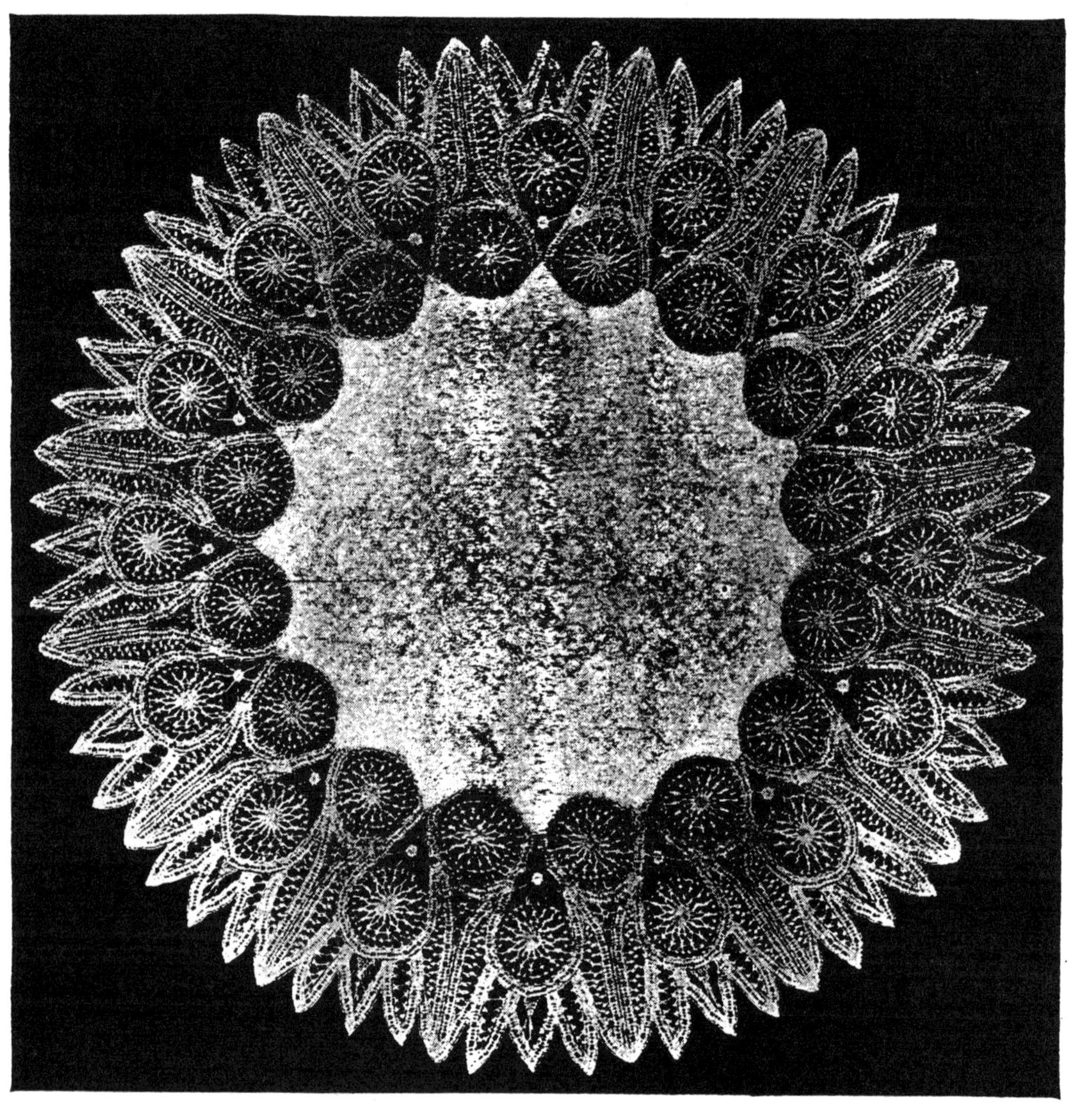

Centre piece of linen, with border of Teneriffe wheels and braid.

Suggestions for the Use of Teneriffe Lace

THE following ideas have been gathered from the best makers of women's apparel both here and abroad; they are taken from work which is being done in constantly increasing amount and are not the mere speculation of what the wheels or medallions might be used for.

A medallion made of fine wool is one of the garnishes for dresses and coats that promises to become extremely popular. A beautiful effect is obtained by doing the knotting in silk.

A ground work laid in white silk and the pattern woven in black; this especially in the close woven patterns, makes a rich ornament for garments of black silken material, and enables one to possess an exclusive trimming which cannot be purchased ready for use.

A trimming for handkerchiefs made of linen thread from the more open or lace-like designs. These may be used in several rows of different diameters or combined with braid in Renaissance designs.

As a border for veils, make the wheels of silk, using a closely twisted silk for the purpose.

Rosettes made of closely twisted silk woven in the more solid designs form a beautiful trimming for evening waists. Irregular outlines may be produced by leaving out some of the threads in laying the ground, as suggested in some of the designs.

Borders are made of lace wheels for cushion tops, doilies, scarfs, centre pieces, tray covers, bureau scarfs, curtains, etc.

For a Baby's Cap.—Baste the wheels on a muslin pattern, and after joining them remove the pattern and sew the crown into the straight front. Finish off the edges with lace.

Rows of small wheels make a beautiful insertion for underwear; and wheels of various sizes are readily adapted to all garments requiring a trimming of lace.

Patterns on blue muslin are procurable in nearly all localities for articles to be worked with braid in combination with lace wheels.

There are patterns of elaborate designs for table linens; pieces for all occasions and services—luncheon cloths, doilies, centre pieces, etc. There are also numerous designs for articles of wearing apparel—such as capes, collars of various shapes and dimensions, yokes, stoles, etc. There are also patterns of borders for gowns, for curtains, bureau scarfs, and some of the prettiest are those for handkerchiefs.

In fact there is scarcely an article for which patterns may not be obtained utilizing lace wheels as the principal element in the design, and in combination with braid and stitches.

Among the articles used in making Teneriffe lace may be mentioned linen thread, crochet cotton, mercerized cotton, Saxony wool, embroidery silk, etc.

Teneriffe lace work.

Teneriffe lace is a kind of work long known in Southern and Central America under the name of Brazilian or Bolivian lace. It is an imitation of a kind of needlework cultivated in Spain in the 16th and 17th centuries and known as "Sols" (Sun lace).

Originally "Sol lace" was made on a linen ground and ranked as "openwork on linen". Little by little, however, a change took place in the mode of its execution and what we now in Europe call "Teneriffe" lace is no longer made on a linen foundation but is properly speaking a lace.

Implements. — These are of various kinds: cushions, metal or india rubber discs, &c.

For our patterns we have used india rubber ones with serrated edges in metal.

Figure 1 represents on a reduced scale a disc of this kind, one side of which is covered with a layer of dark cloth to make it less trying for the eyes in working. The little metal teeth serve to keep the threads tightly stretched for the web.

The bigger circular discs have the same serrated outside rims which admit of a greater number of threads being used for the web.

For the insertions, braids and lace edgings, special moulds are used of the shape and size to suit the work in hand.

Needles. — There are special needles for Teneriffe lace; they are very long, of uniform thickness and without points. They are slightly curved and flattened at the extremity which admits of lifting up the threads of the web more easily.

Materials. — These must be selected with a view to the purpose the work is intended to serve. For trimming articles of dress requiring a fine lace, use the finer numbers of Flax thread for lace D.M.C (Lin pour dentelles) or Alsatian thread D.M.C (Fil d'Alsace) in white, cream or écru; for table or bed linen, we recommend the coarser numbers of Crochet cotton, 6 cord D.M.C (Cordonnet 6 fils) and Flax thread for knitting D.M.C (Lin à tricoter); for coloured braids use Pearl cotton D.M.C (Coton perlé).

The above-named articles serve to form the stretched web and the knots that hold and fix it; where the pattern requires ornamental figures in darning stitch use a loose thread such as Special stranded cotton D.M.C (Mouliné spécial), Stranded flax thread D.M.C (Lin mouliné) or Persian silk D.M.C (Soie de Perse).

After stretching the threads over the disc make the rows of knots that complete the web, beginning at the outside edge, then furnish the centre and lastly make the different ornamental stitches.

To renew your thread make a weaver's knot which must come quite close to a knot of the web or be hidden under a little ornamental figure.

How to stretch the web for the wheels (figures 1, 2 and 3). — With the thread unwinding from the ball make a knotted loop at the bottom, as long as half the diameter of the disc to be covered and hook it round one of the teeth. The knot of the loop will thus just come in the centre of the made round and there will be an end of thread beside the knot, which, later on, will serve for fastening off the thread last stretched.

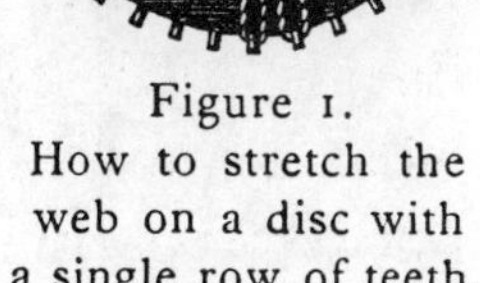

Figure 1.
How to stretch the web on a disc with a single row of teeth.

Take the thread of the ball in the right hand and carrying it across the disc hook it on to the opposite tooth. Then take it upwards again to the next tooth and so on till all the teeth are occupied (figure 1) and the central space is entirely covered with threads. Lastly fasten the thread to the loose end of thread of the first loop by a weaver's knot.

The big discs, the inside rims of which are serrated outside and inside are covered in two rounds. The first time (figure 2) you carry your thread zigzag over each of the inside teeth and over every alternate outside tooth; on the second round (figure 3) the thread is stretched across the disc round the teeth left free before.

How to make the web for insertions and lace. — For these the threads can be mounted in one or two rounds. In the former case take one tooth above and one below in succession; in the latter, carry the thread on the first round only over each alternate tooth, and on the second, over all the teeth left free the first time. The two layers of threads, one above the other, will cross each other quite naturally in the centre of the disc.

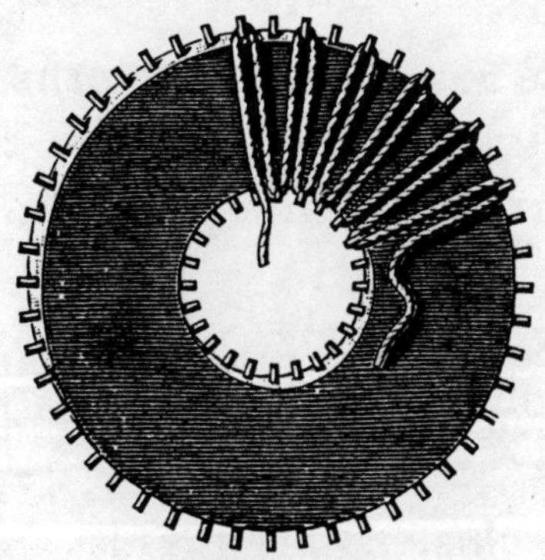

Figure 2.
How to stretch the web on a disc with serrated rims inside and outside.
First round.

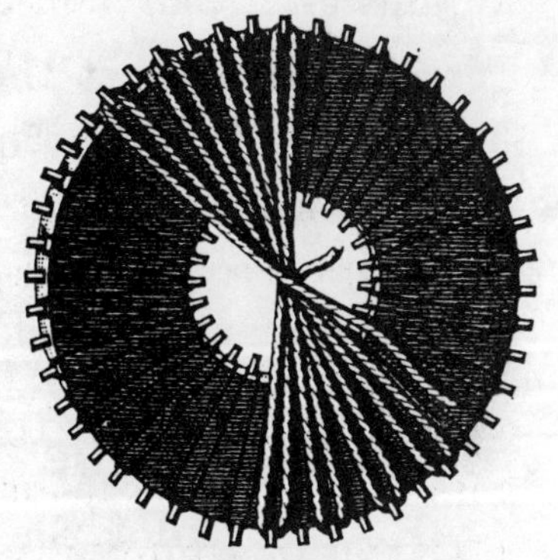

Figure 3.
How to stretch the web on a disc with serrated rims inside and outside.
Second round.

How to make the knots that fix the stretched threads in place (figures 4 and 5). — To complete the web make several rows of knots which kepp the stretched threads in place.

You can knot each thread separately or collect two or more by one knot. You make the same kind of knots as in drawn thread work on linen: the collecting knot formed by a small double chain stitch (figure 4) and the single twisted knot (figure 5).

In making the first row of knots you form at the same time the little outside scallops; the next rows arranged in different ways, partly form the pattern.

By making successive rows of knots over the same threads of the web you get between these rows small square spaces, by alternating the knots, that is to say, dividing between them the clusters of threads that come from a preceding row you form a sort

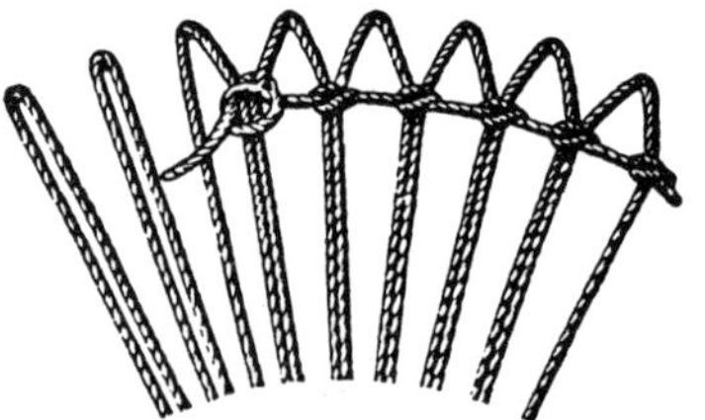

Figure 4.
Knot in chain stitch twistet contrariwise.

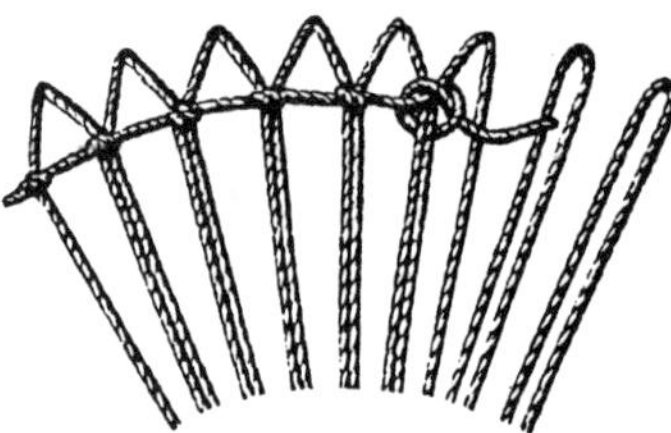

Figure 5.
Single chain stitch twisted one way.

of waved line and the joining together of several clusters of threads produces patterns on a big scale.

In a single pattern you can use these three kinds of collecting knots, as the engravings shew.

How to ornament the centre of the wheels. — The centre of the wheels where the stretched threads meet is always ornamented by a small spider. This is made in darning or in ribbed stitch whichever best suits the other parts of the pattern with which it should always agree.

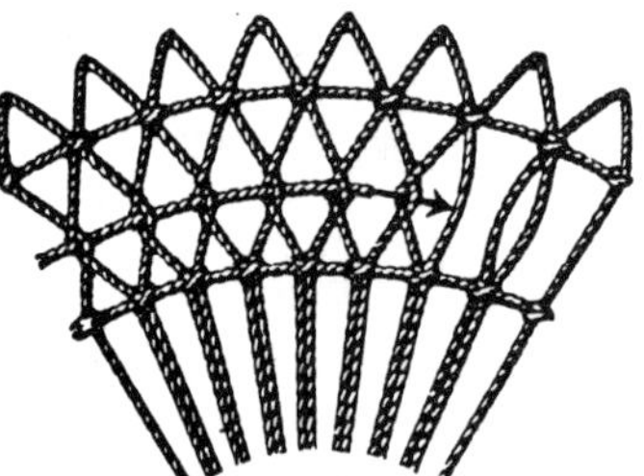

Figure 6.
Row of threads set once contrariwise.

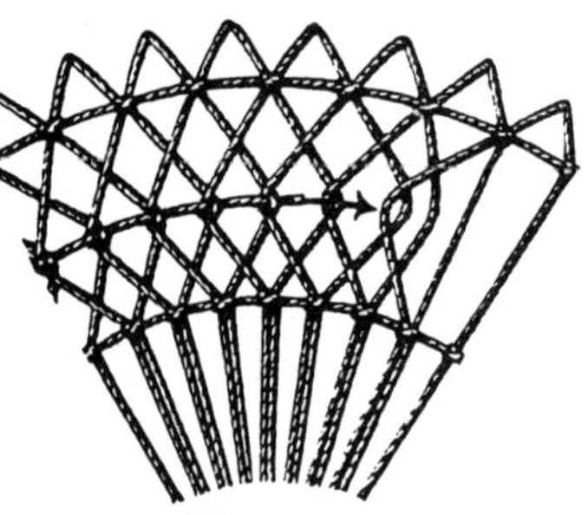

Figure 7.
Row of threads set once contrariwise.

Ornamental stitches and figures. — After you have made all the rows of knots and the spider in the middle of the wheel, the preparatory work is finished. For filling the empty spaces you can use any of the various stitches used in openwork on linen; very pretty effects are produced with the different rows of threads drawn opposite ways finished off top and bottom by a row of small wheels, darning or buttonhole stitches. A very handsome effect is obtained with scallops and festons in darning stitch.

How to cellect the clusters of threads contrariwise one row beneth the other (figures 6 and 7). — The threads must be drawn together contrariwise in each row in the same way as in the rows of openwork; in fact all the motives and stitches used in openwork on linen can be used for Teneriffe lace.

As explanatory details we give in figure 6 the simplest row formed by two threads set once contrariwise, whilst figure 7 shows the execution of a row where the threads are set twice contrariwise.

How to knot the clusters of threads. — Usually the clusters of threads are knotted together by executing the rows of knots which fix the web. Anyway the model sometimes requires that the clusters should form a pattern that has a waved line in the middle. In this case the first cluster that is already knotted must be divided and your thread twisted once or twice round half the threads of the cluster until you come to the first part of the next cluster; then you join the two parts, carry your thread to the next part and so on.

Wheels. — The ornamental motive most often used in this kind of work is the wheel or spider.

It is worked in darning stitch, either single or set contrariwise or in ribbed stitch.

The different kinds of wheels are so much used in every kind of embroidery that we think they will be familiar to all our readers, and therefore shall not enter here into any fuller description of the same.

Circles, braids, scallops and festons in darning stitch (figures 8, 9 and 10). — Teneriffe lace, where a less transparent effect is desired, and which seems to demand the

Figure 8.
Braid in darning stitch.

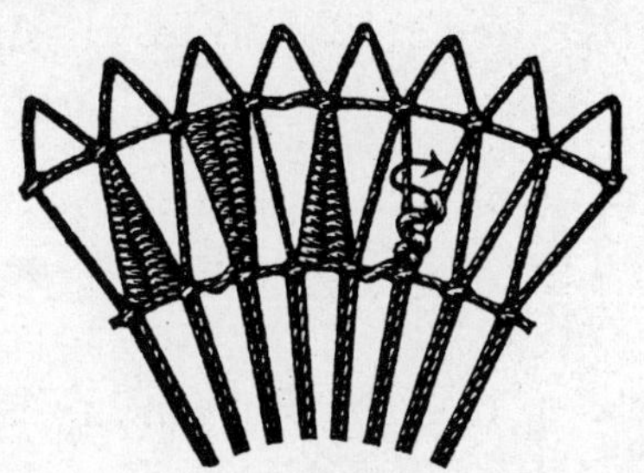

Figure 9.
Scallops in darning stitch.

Figure 10.
Festons in darning stitch.

introduction of several colours should le filled in with circles, or braids in darning stitch. The empty spaces, between two rows of knots, should be entirely filled with rows of darning stitches set different ways (figure 8).

The scallops in darning stitch (figure 9) are always begun at the point and worked in the ordinary way; the thread, which should, as far as possible, remain hidden is taken from one scallop to the other over the threads of the web.

Figure 10 shows the working of the festons in darning stitch, for which the needle is carried to and fro over several threads of the web, the ends of which meet in a knot.

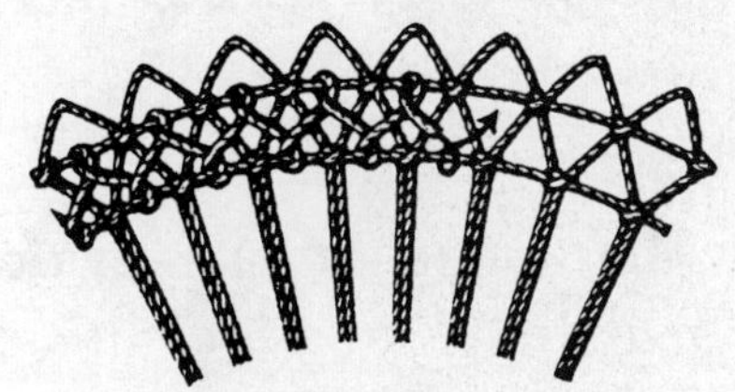

Figure 11.
Band in Russian stitch.

Chains in Russian and button-hole stitch, bars of stretched threads (figure 11). — The intervals, in the shape of triangles or squares, produced by two rows of knots, made over the threads of the web, giving rather a poor effect, often need ornamenting with a filling stitch, by preference Russian stitch (figure 11).

In certain cases one may make a row of loops in button-hole stitch or bars of threads stretched singly, resting on the knotted rows.

Detailed descriptions of the different lace stitches and ornamental figures will be found in the following works of the D.M.C Library: *Encyclopedia of Needlework (Encyclopédie des Ouvrages de Dames), Renaissance Lace (La Dentelle Renaissance), Embroidered Net (Le Filet brodé), Openwork on Net (Jours sur Toile).*

How to take the work when finished off the india rubber disc. This is done by carefully lifting each little scallop with a blunt needle from each tooth and slipping it carefully over the metal tooth.

The metal discs are furnished with a mechanism by which the work can be taken off by a very simple movement.

Imitation done with Teneriffe braids. — Besides the Teneriffe lace made entirely by hand on metal or india rubber discs it can be imitated in a special kind of braid called Teneriffe braid. These braids consist of a narrow openwork gimp, with small picots at the bottom and a row of long loops at the top, collected together by a coarse thread drawn through them to keep them in place. To make the pattern this thread is drawn out and the loops freed.

They are then collected together in different clusters to form wheels, insertions and laces, and replace the hand-made web of stretched threads.

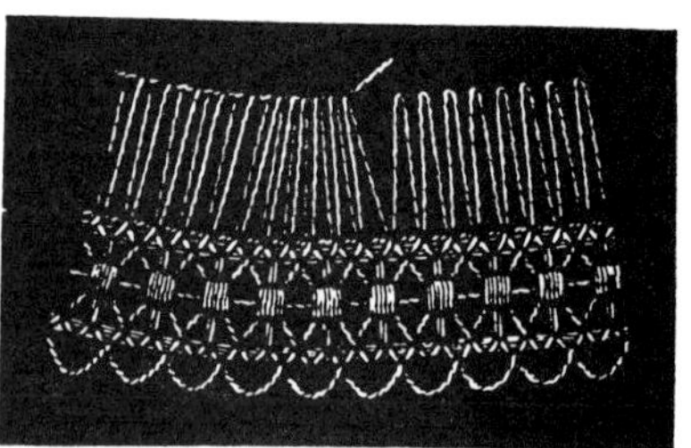

Figure 12.
Pattern of Ténériffe lace.

Materials (figure 12. — The Teneriffe braids (see figure 12) are made in several sizes and patterns, in white and écru; they are to be had at the needlework shops. For drawing the loops of thread together use Flax thread for lace D.M.C (Lin pour dentelles) or Alsatian thread D.M.C (Fil d'Alsace) in Nos 50, 60 or 70; the same are also used for the different lace stitches and should always exactly match the braid in colour.

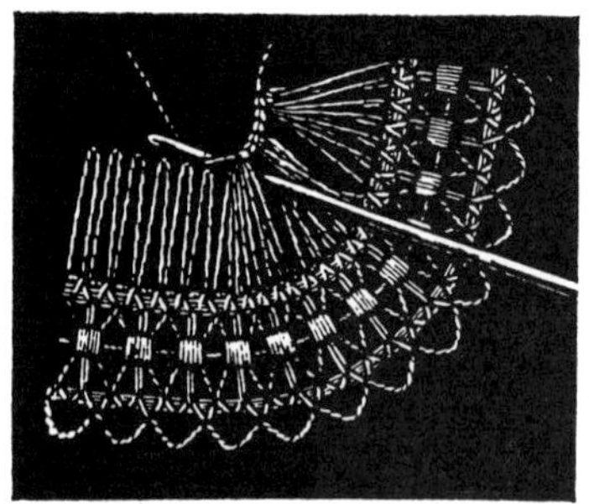

Figure 13.
Clusters of loops connected by a single stitch.

Some ornamental stitches and the decorative figures which should stand out prominently on the foundation web of threads should be done with Pearl cotton D.M.C (Coton perlé) in No 3, 5 or 8 and if advisable in a different colour from the braid.

Patterns. — The lace made with Teneriffe braid has to be made after traced patterns like those used for Renaissance lace.

These will show by a double line the place for the braid and by small strokes on the outer line, where the little scallops are to come that form the finish. Any other indications inside the circle, bands or festons are superfluous.

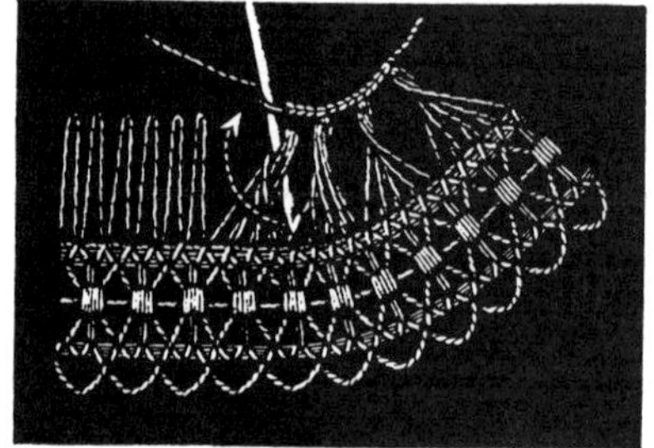

Figure 14.
Loops joined by a plain stitch in clusters twisted once.

How to crochet together the loops of the braid (figures 13 and 14). — After having drawn out the thread that holds the loops (see figure 12), you collect these latter in the number of clusters indicated by the pattern you are copying.

This is most easily done with a crochet needle; in figure 13 the loops mounted on the crochet needle are joined together by a single stitch, whilst figure 14 shows how to twist the cluster of loops once round itself. The clusters may also be crossed one over the other and so on.

In the little wheels the clusters touch in the middle; in the big ones, in insertions and in lace the intervals are indispensable and the connection between the clusters is made by means of small chains of chain stiches.

Tacking on the braids. — The pieces of braid with the loops connected by crochet are laid on the pattern, wrong side uppermost and fastened down by stitches that fix each loop of the braid in the place indicated on the pattern by a small stroke.

The pieces of braid and thread should be sewn down as carefully as possible, the inside edge of the braid must then be gathered by means of overcasting stitches so that the fulness be equally distributed and the braid lie perfectly flat.

Making the lace stitches. — You begin by making the rays, the rings and the festons that form the web of the work.

Upon these principal figures you then embroider the ornamental stitches and lastly you cross and knot the clusters of loops.

How to detach the lace when finished from the pattern. — When the work is finished iron it with a moderately hot iron, then detach it from the pattern by cutting the tacking stitches at the back; pull out the ends of thread and the lace will come off of itself.

Plates 1 to 20. — The following plates contain a series of different patterns, representing the principal types of Teneriffe lace, some done entirely by hand the others with Teneriffe braids.

Plate 2

Plate 4

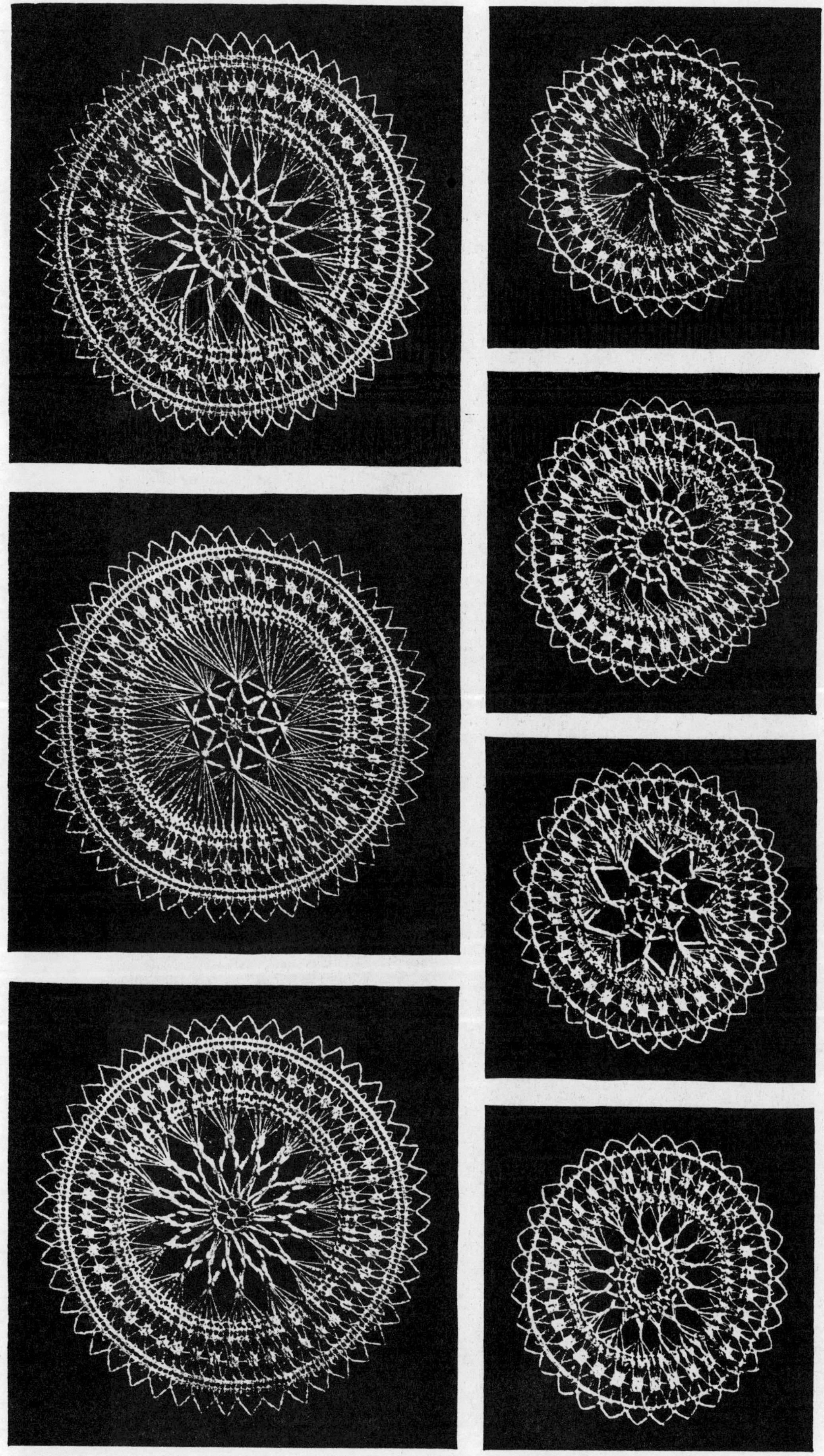

Plate 6

Plate 7

Plate 8

Plate 10

Plate 12

Plate 13

Plate 14

Plate 16

Plate 17

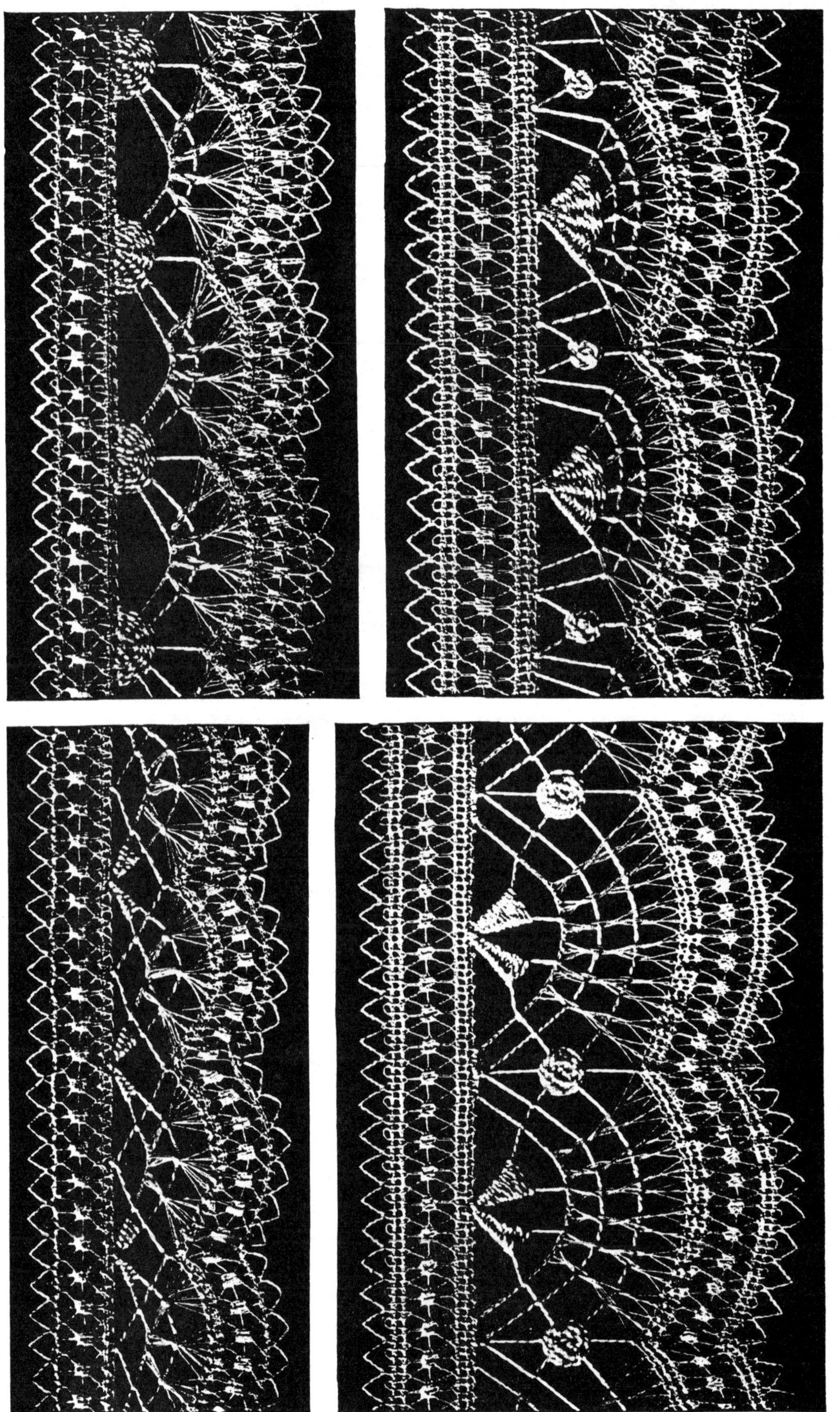

Plate 18

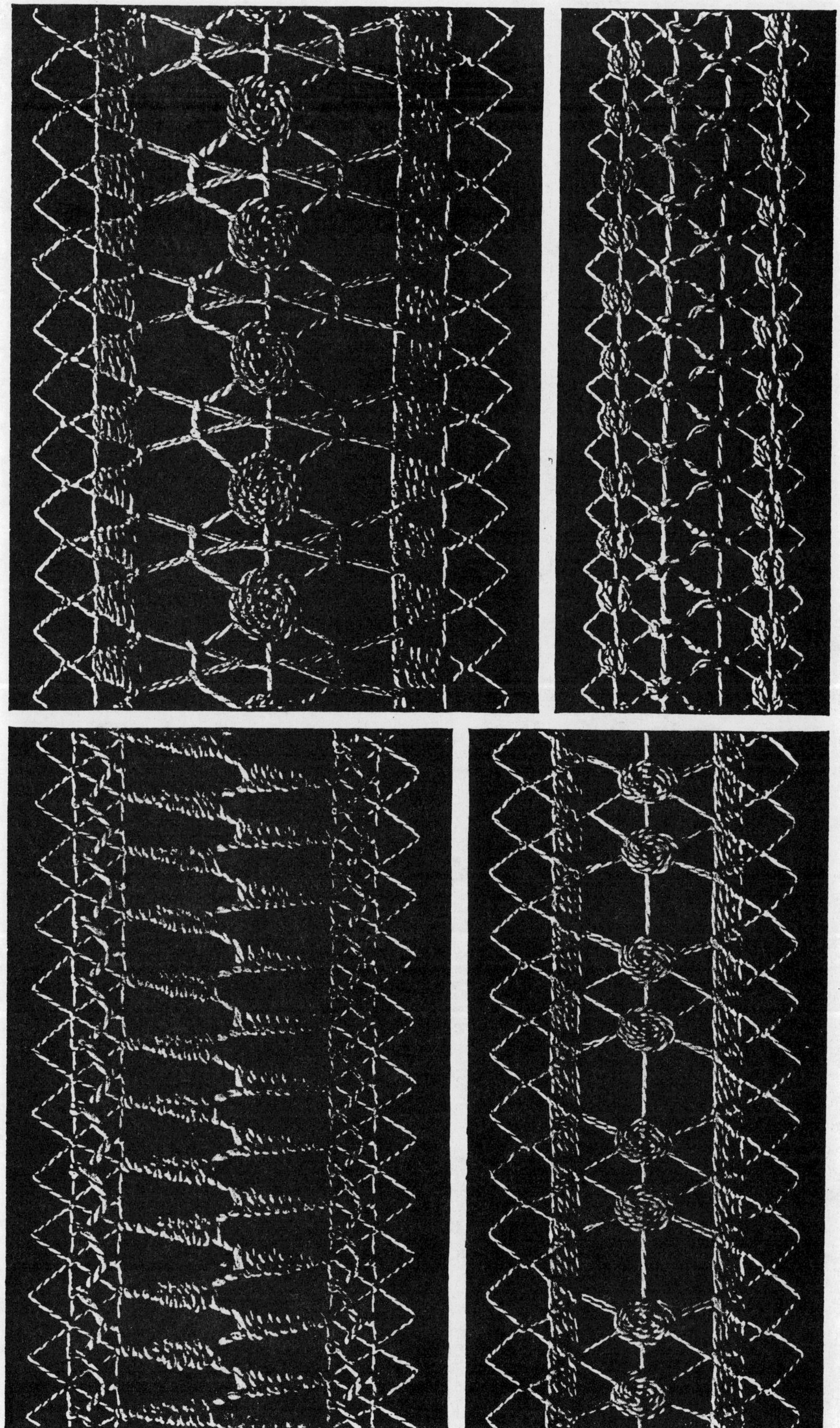

Plate 19

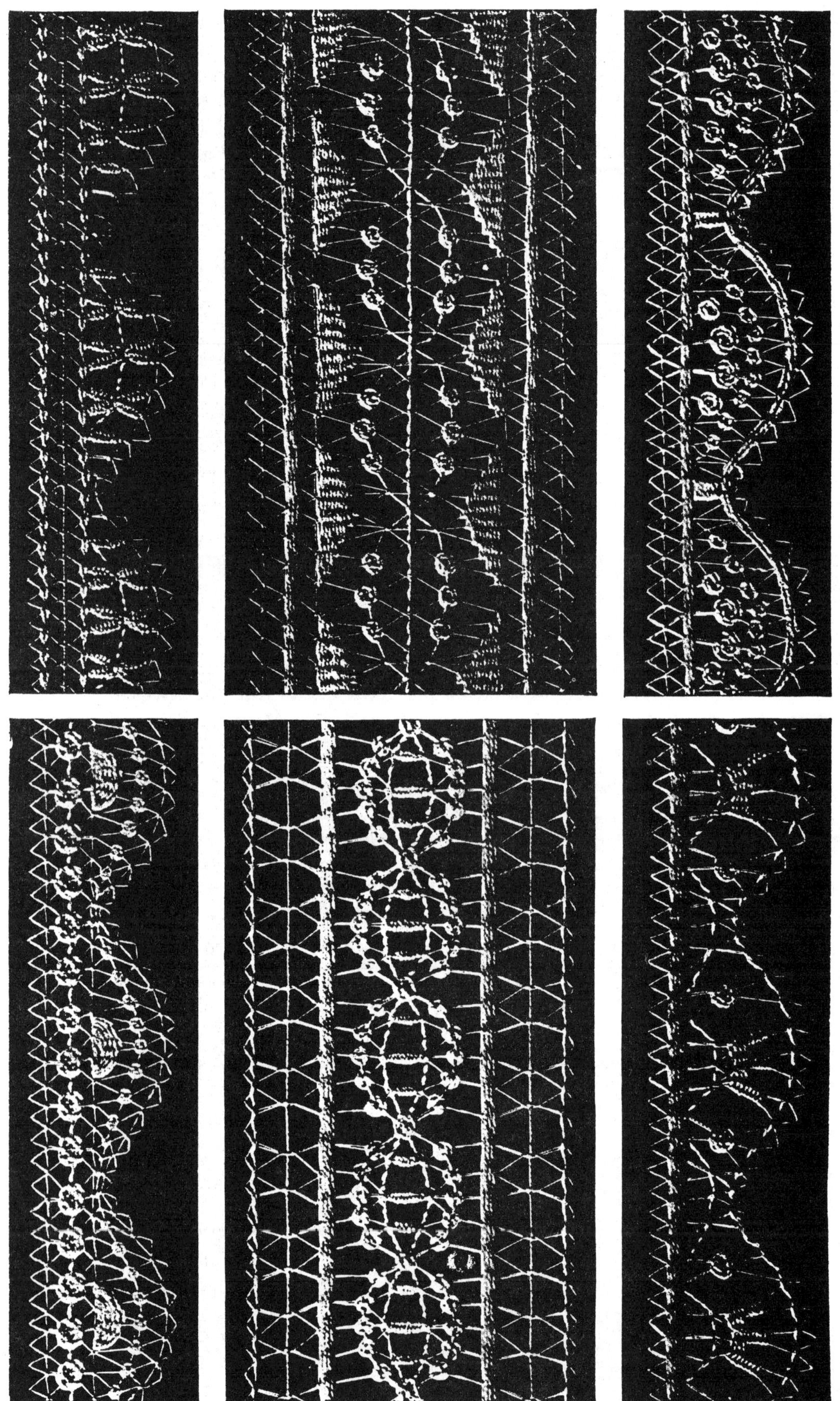

Plate 20

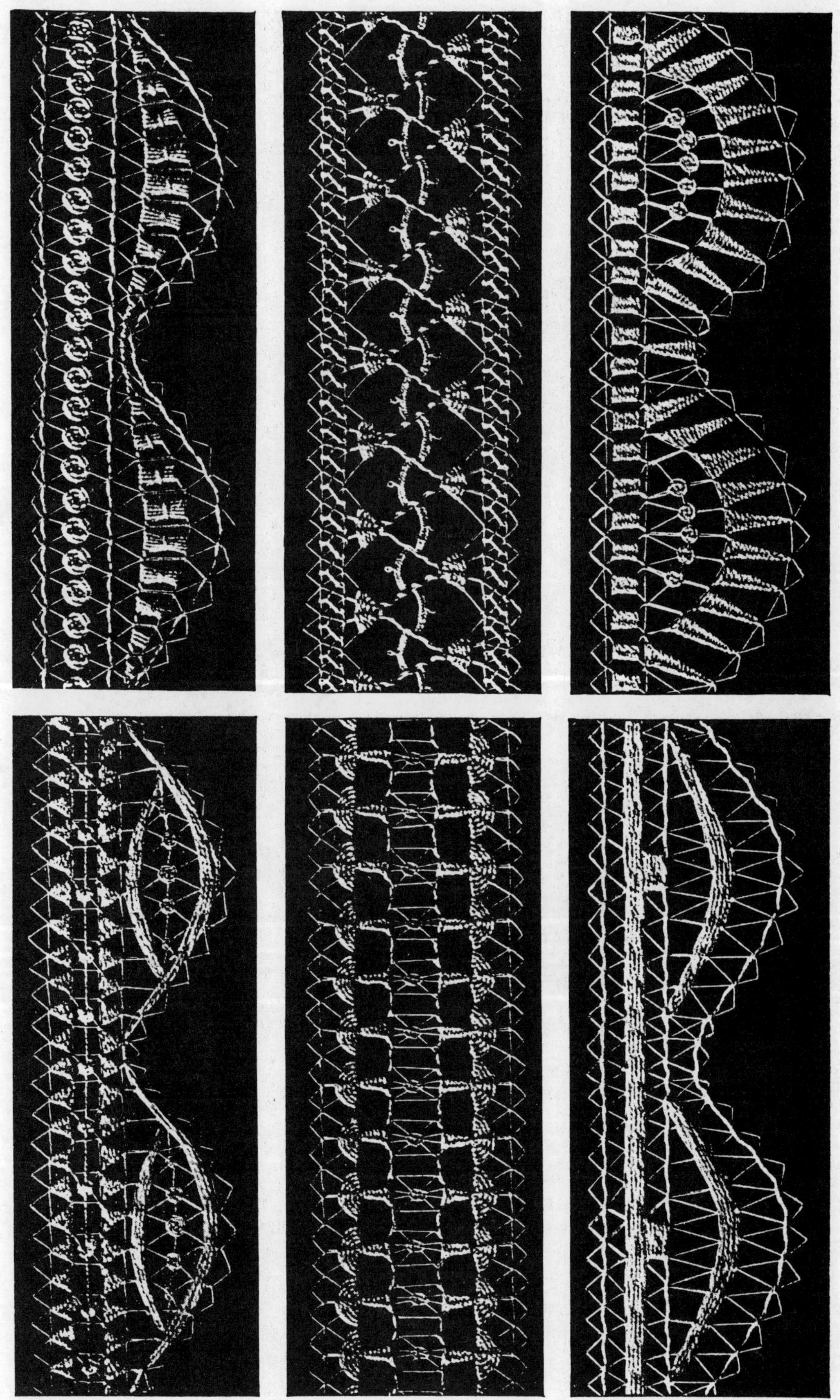

Lace Making.

Teneriffe Lace.

TENERIFFE lace takes its name from Teneriffe Island, the largest of the islands forming the Canary group in the North Atlantic Ocean. Taoro, a name applied to the wheels, is a sacred valley in Teneriffe, where, in the fifteenth century, and even earlier, much of this lace was made. Another name by which the lace is called is Brazilian point, and a great deal of it is made to-day in Brazil and in other South American countries. The women of Teneriffe were probably the first to make these beautiful wheels, which are now being used for decorating dresses and coats for women and children, and also for making stole or bishop stocks, cuffs, etc.

The lace is suitable also for center pieces, doilies, bureau scarfs and tea cloths, and for borders for luncheon and dinner cloths.

FIGURE NO. 1.—BERTHA IN TENERIFFE LACE.

It is not possible to give a lesson on every design of wheel that can be made, but after the placing of the threads on the cushion has been mastered (see Figures Nos. 3, 4 and 5) one may work out new designs in unlimited variety as their fancy may impel.

In the bertha (Figure No. 1) are used wheels of several designs in various sizes. One of these is the wheel shown in Figure No. 2. It is worked on a cushion like that shown at Figure No. 5. An even number of pins are always used. For this wheel forty-eight are needed, and are arranged at regular intervals around the circumference of wheel in cushion, the heads of pins raised about one-fourth of an inch. Four yards of thread are needed to make one wheel. Take end of thread in left hand, holding same at center of wheel; pass thread

FIGURE NO. 2.
WHEEL USED IN BERTHA.

around pin No. 1 and carry over to pin 25, being careful to hold end of thread at center with the left hand. Carry thread back to No. 2, and from No. 2 to No. 26, and from No. 3 to No. 27; and so on until you have passed it around pins 24 and 48, these completing the wheel. Bring thread in right hand to center and tie to the end held in left hand, thus securing the thread. Now press pins down close to cushion to hold thread in place while weaving. Use a large, pointless needle. Start weaving by passing over and under threads alternately to the fifth thread (see Figure No. 4); then with point of needle work the thread down so that it rests as near the center of the work as possible. Continue in this manner three times around. You will know when you complete the first round, as you will then have to skip a thread to start the weaving of the second row on account of the even number of pins; otherwise you would be weaving on the same thread.

FIGURE NO. 4.
SQUARE. WORK COMMENCED.

The third row of weaving completed, take one stitch toward the center to fasten the weaving securely. Here, without cutting thread, start the forming of spokes to the wheel, as in No. 2 by placing needle under single thread on pin No. 1 and also under three double threads and one single thread, taking half from pin No. 1 and half from pin No. 5. Allow your needle to come through the loop in thread and pull so that when the thread is drawn up it will form a tight knot. After this first spoke is finished, take the single thread left on pin No. 5 and the three double threads following it; also the single thread on pin No. 9. Draw these up and fasten in a knot, allowing needle first to pass through the loop as before. Repeat this until all the spokes are formed and you will have just twelve completed spokes.

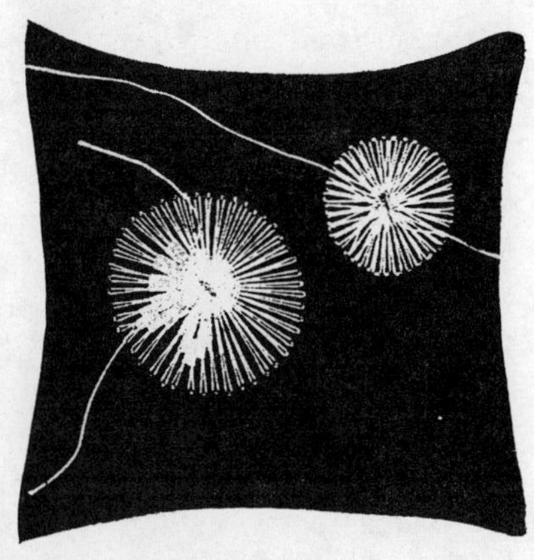

FIGURE NO. 3.
WHEELS PARTLY WORKED.

Now start to weave—by placing your needle under one thread and over the next at the ends of the spokes the same as in the beginning, until you have completed four rows of weaving. This done you start a row of knots outside of the weaving, leaving a short space between. Commence on pin No. 1, taking one

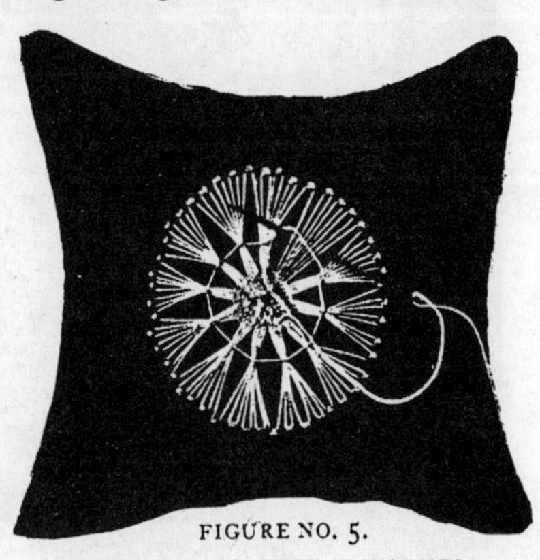

FIGURE NO. 5.
SHOWING HOW KNOT IS WORKED.

thread from pin No. 1 and one from pin No. 2, pass needle through the loop of the thread and pull up tight to knot. Take thread left on pin No. 2 and the single thread on pin No. 3, doing as before and forming a second knot. Continue until circle is completed. In the same manner make another row of knots outside the first and quite close to the pins at margin. This last forms the picots on edge of wheel. This done take out the pins from cushion and remove the lace.

When one wheel is completed you will be anxious to go on and will find the work very fascinating as you see it grow under your fingers.

FIGURE NO. 6.
SHOWING USE OF FIGURES NOS. 7 AND 8.

FIGURE NO. 7.
SQUARE FOR COLLAR, FIGURE NO. 6.

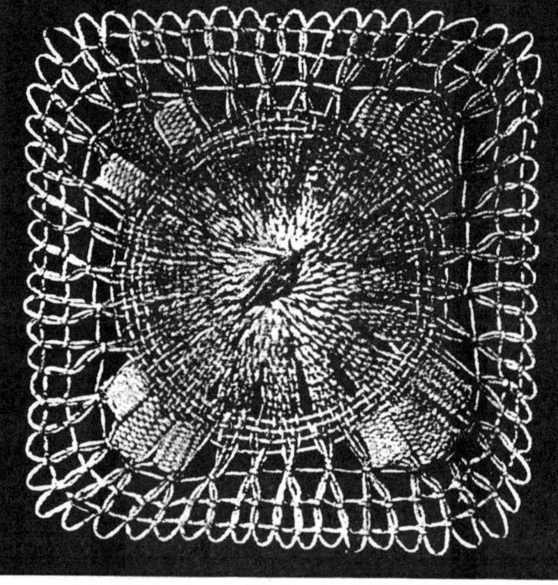

FIGURE NO. 8.
SQUARE FOR COSTUME, FIGURE NO. 6.

In working the squares the pins are of course placed on the cushion in a square form —not round (see Figure No. 4). For this large square sixty-eight pins are used. On account of its large size, the thread cannot readily be measured in advance. The thread is passed from pin to pin in the same manner as in the round medallion just described. The center is worked similarly, having three rows of weaving. The threads are divided in sections by taking from five pins at one corner of the design. The corners only are treated in this way. On the sides the threads are taken from three pins. This will give twenty-four spokes to the wheel. Each spoke must be woven about six times. Of course the weaving is done on ten threads at the corner, six threads being woven together on the sides until the twenty-four spokes are finished.

After this start and take up every other thread making four rows of weaving — then from the corner you weave six rows and ten threads again, and on four threads either side of the ten. After the four corners are worked in this manner, make a row of knots by taking up four threads, a single thread from pin No. 1, the two threads from pin No. 2, and a single thread from pin No. 3, drawing needle through the loop and pulling to a tight knot.

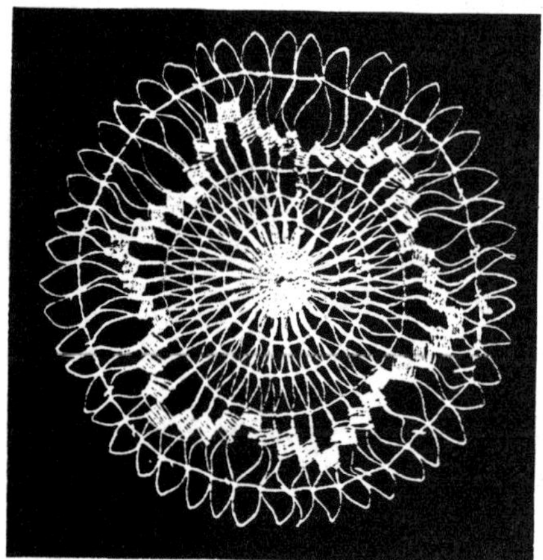

FIGURE NO. 9.
WHEEL FOR SCARF. SEE FIGURES NOS. 15 AND 16 ON PAGE 37.

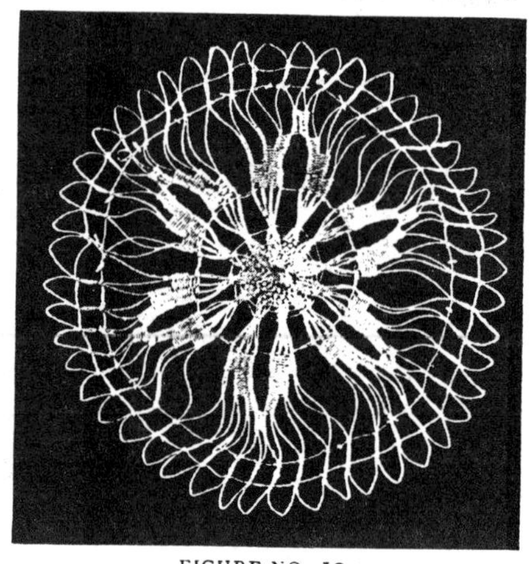

FIGURE NO. 10.
WHEEL FOR PILLOW, FIGURE NO. 18.

Repeat in this manner until row is completed. Other knotted rows are made according to illus-

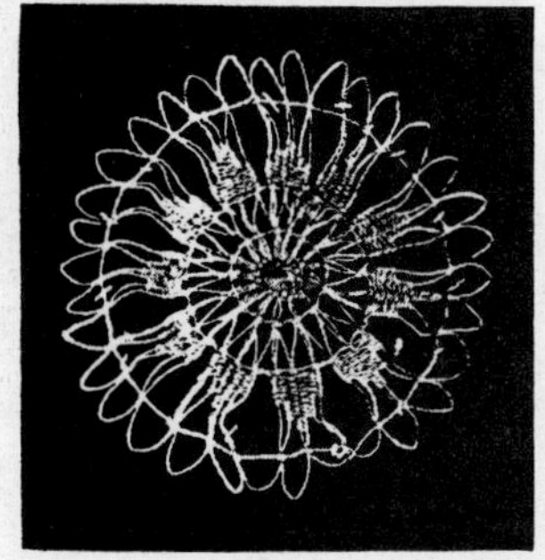

FIGURE NO. 12.
FOR CORNERS OF PILLOW, FIGURE NO. 18.

tration No. 4, the last being made nearest the edge.

The squares illustrated are worked with very heavy linen thread in white or

FIGURE NO. 11.
HOW FIGURE NO. 13 IS USED.

colors to suit the color of gown to be decorated. Squares like Figure No. 7 are used in the bishop stock collar in costume, Figure No. 6. Squares decorate the same costume which may be made either of white, blue, or grass colored linen. Wheels No. 9 and 10 are used in bertha Figure No. 1, page 22, and bureau scarf, Figure No. 16, page 37, respectively.

FIGURE NO. 13.
WAIST TRIMMING.

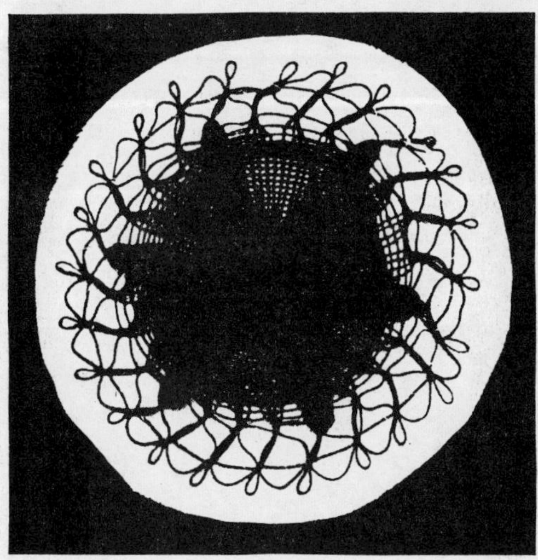

FIGURE NO. 14.
MEDALLION.

We need now to explain, having described the making of the wheels, how they are associated in the bertha shown at Figure No. 1 and in the other Teneriffe pieces illustrated in this number.

The usual cambric pattern is not needed for these pieces, as no braid is to be used with the wheels. It is advisable, however, to have a paper pattern cut to the size and shape of the trimming it is proposed to make. A stiff brown paper is best for this purpose.

After this is prepared for the bertha, say, baste the wheels on it, beginning at the center and working out towards the edges and ends, placing the wheels so they will present an attractive uniform design. Use care in basting or the wheels will shift and spoil the work. It is well to first lay out the wheels on the paper pattern to get the best effect, pinning them to the place before any basting is done. The basting completed, the wheels should be joined together where they meet with simple lace knots and the spaces should be filled with the Brussels net stitch, or any other simple stitch which may be preferred. It is not advisable to use any elaborate stitches as the effect would be lost.

These directions will apply also to the other Teneriffe pieces shown in this number, and to all Teneriffe lace combinations where braid is not used.

If braid is used it is necessary to have the usual cambric pattern on which both braid and wheels are basted and the spaces may then be filled with a variety of stitches.

The lesson in the March number of THE LACE MAKER will be on Bruges Lace, how to make it and the various ways of using it.

Thesa
Handarbeitsbuch
für
Spitzen, Sterne, Einsätze
* in leichtester Ausführung *

Die Abbildungen der Thesa-Formen.

Die nachfolgenden Abbildungen veranschaulichen die Thesa-Formen in $^1/_2$ natürlicher Größe.
Nähere Angaben auf der 4. Umschlagseite.

Satz I. Rund.

Nr. 1.
3 cm Durchmesser.
24 Einschnitte.

Nr. 2.
5 cm Durchmesser.
36 und 48 Einschn.

Nr. 3.
8 cm Durchmesser.
48 und 60 Einschn.

Nr. 4.
12 cm Durchmesser.
72 Einschnitte.

Satz II. Dreieck.

Nr. 5.
$4^1/_2$ cm Durchm.,
39 Einschnitte.

Nr. 6.
$5^1/_2$ cm Durchm.,
54 Einschnitte.

Nr. 7.
7 cm Durchmesser.
72 Einschnitte.

Nr. $7^1/_2$.
11 cm Durchmesser.
102 Einschnitte.

Satz I.

Satz I.

Satz IV.

Satz II. Nr. $7^1/_2$.

Satz II.

Satz III.

Satz III.

Satz IV. Achteck.

Nr. 11.
4 cm Durchmesser,
40 Einschnitte.

Nr. 12.
$5^1/_2$ cm Durchm.,
64 Einschnitte.

Nr. 13.
$8^1/_2$ cm Durchm.,
96 Einschnitte.

❖

Satz III. Viereck.

Nr. 8.
4 cm Durchmesser,
24 und 44 Einschn.

Nr. 9.
7 cm Durchmesser,
48 und 92 Einschn.

Nr. 10.
12 cm Durchmesser,
136 Einschnitte.

❖

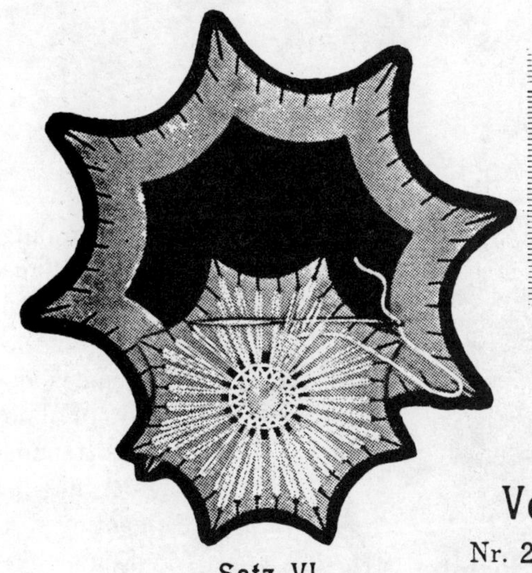
Satz VI.

Satz VI. Stern.

Nr. 16. $5^1/_2$ cm Durchmesser, mit 48 Einschn.

Nr. 17. $9^1/_2$ cm Durchmesser, mit 56 Einschn.

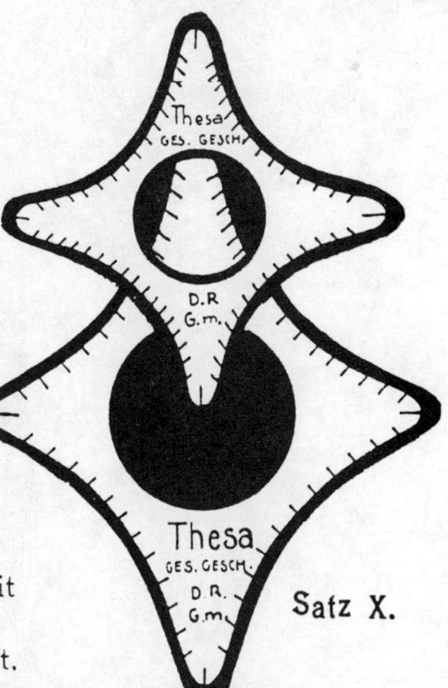

Satz X.

Satz X. Verbindungsformen.

Nr. 25. 12 cm Durchmesser, mit 56 Einschnitten.

Nr. 26. 16 cm lang, 13 cm breit, mit 56 Einschnitten.

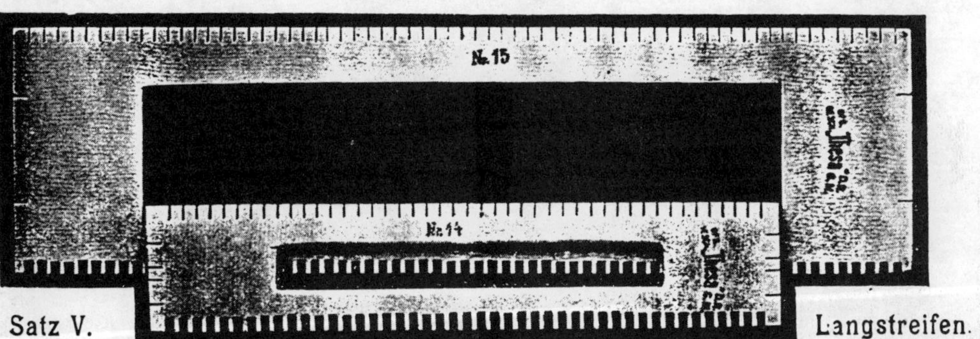

Satz V. Langstreifen.

Nr. 14. 15 cm lang, $3^1/_2$ cm breit.
Nr. 15. 20 cm lang, $5^1/_2$ cm breit.

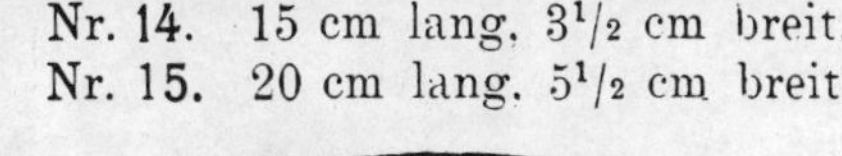

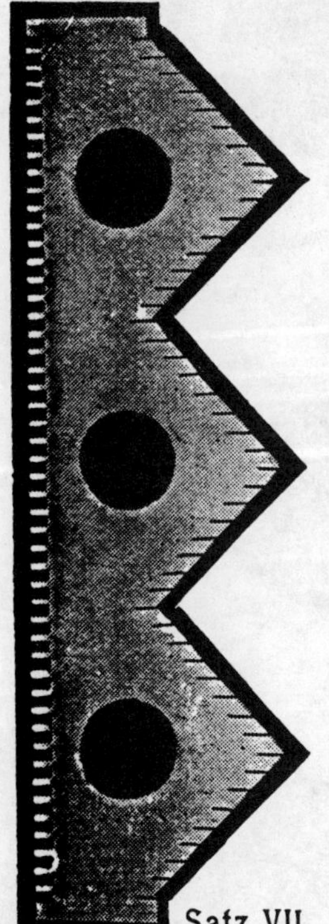
Satz VII.

Gezackter Langstreifen.

Nr. 18. 16 cm lang, $4^1/_2$ cm breit.

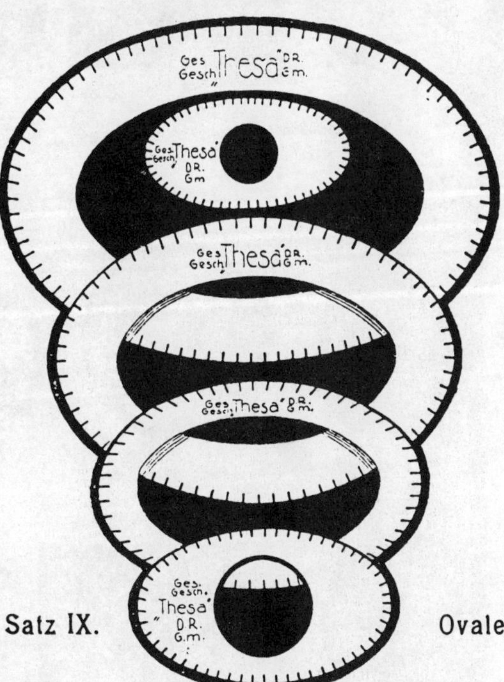

Satz IX. Ovale.

Nr. 20. 10 cm lang, $5^1/_2$ cm breit, 40 Einschn.
Nr. 21. $12^1/_2$ cm lang, 7 cm breit, 48 Einschn.
Nr. 22. 16 cm lang, $9^1/_2$ cm breit, 54 Einschn.
Nr. 23. 19 cm lang, 13 cm breit, 72 Einschn.
Nr. 24. 25 cm lang, $15^1/_2$ cm breit, 84 Einschn.

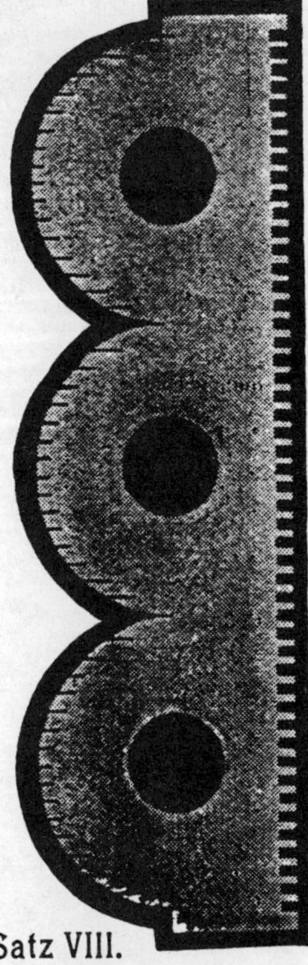
Satz VIII.

Langstreifen mit Bogen.

Nr. 19. 16 cm lang, $4^1/_2$ cm breit.

Muster für Thesa-Formen Nr. 1.

Der Verkauf der hier angegebenen Thesa-Arbeiten erfolgt als naturgroße Photographie, nach der nicht nur die Thesa-Arbeit, sondern auch die event. Häkelumrandg. mühelos ausgeführt werden kann. Ein Zurücksenden der Photographie entfällt und bleibt dieselbe Eigentum des Käufers.

Nr. 1.

Nr. 2.

Nr. 3.

Muster für Thesa-Formen Nr. 2.

Nr. 4.

Nr. 5

Nr. 6.

Nr. 7.

Nr. 8.

Nr. 9.

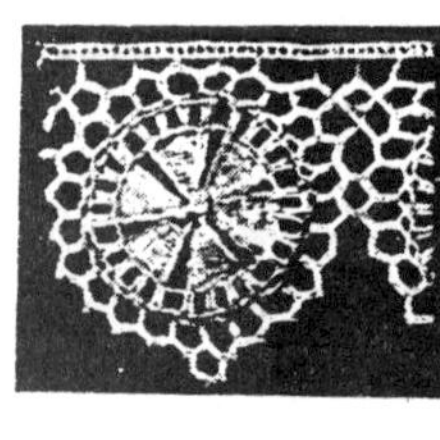
Nr. 10.

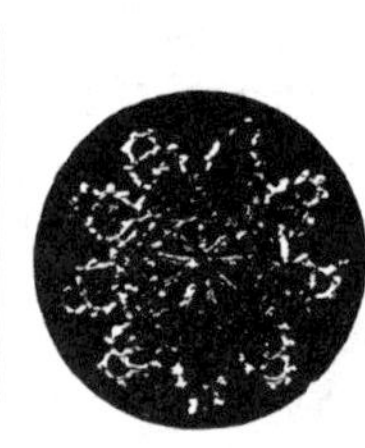
Nr. 11.

Nr. 12.

Muster für Thesa-Formen Nr. 3.

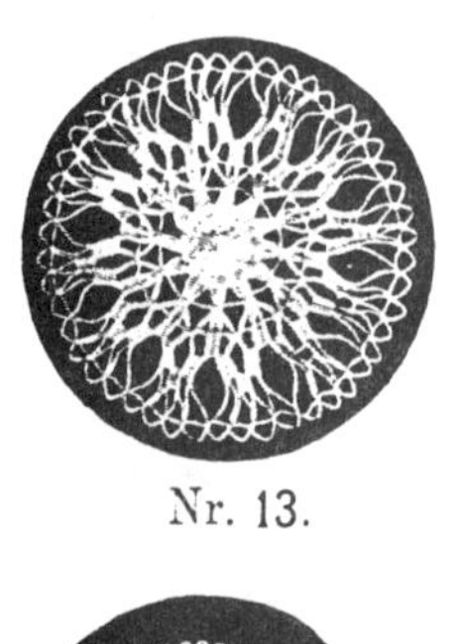
Nr. 13.

Nr. 14.

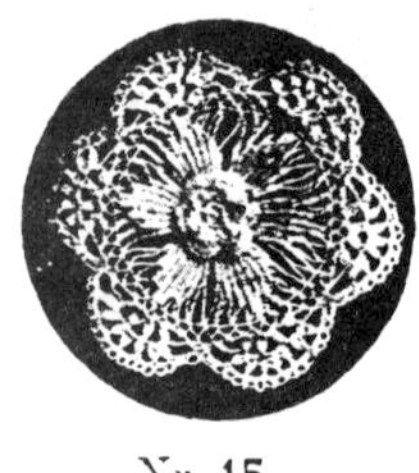
Nr. 15.

Nr. 16.

Nr. 17.

Nr. 18.

Nr. 19.

Nr. 20.

Nr. 21.

Nr. 22.

Muster für Thesa-Formen Nr. 4.

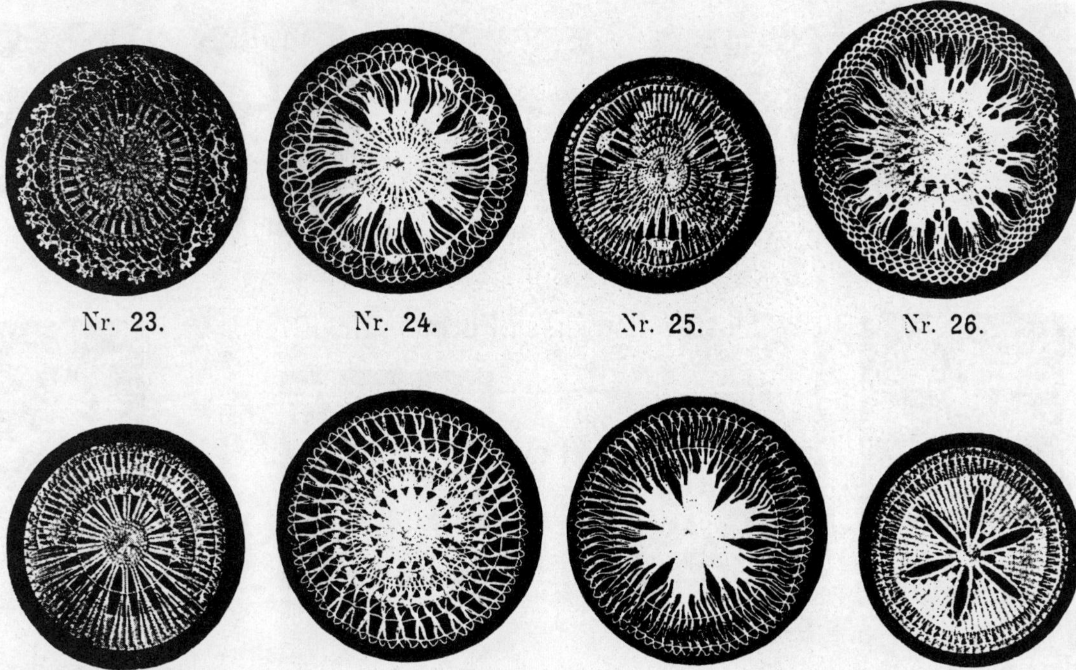

Nr. 23. Nr. 24. Nr. 25. Nr. 26.

Nr. 27. Nr. 28. Nr. 29. Nr. 30.

Thesa-Formen Nr. 5. Thesa-Formen Nr. 6.

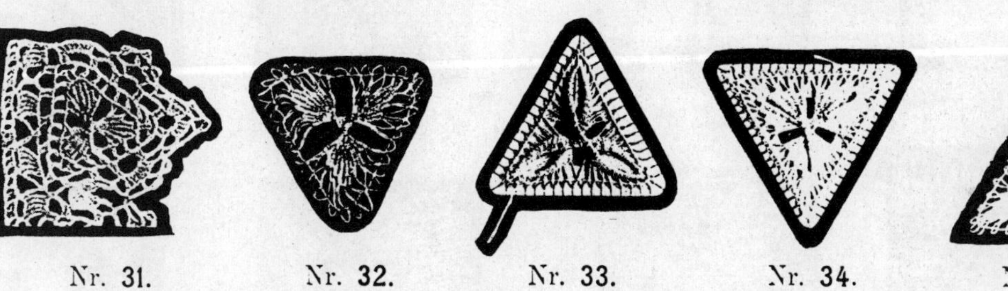

Nr. 31. Nr. 32. Nr. 33. Nr. 34. Nr. 35.

Thesa-Formen Nr. 7. Thesa-Formen Nr. $7^1/_2$.

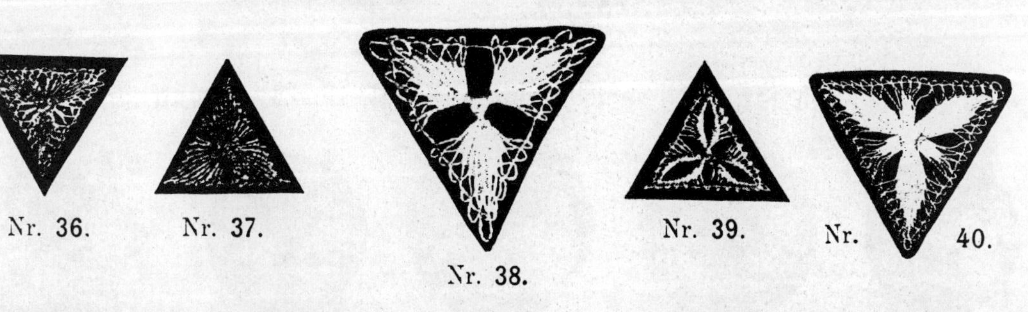

Nr. 36. Nr. 37. Nr. 38. Nr. 39. Nr. 40.

Muster für Thesa-Formen Nr. 8. Thesa-Formen Nr. 9.

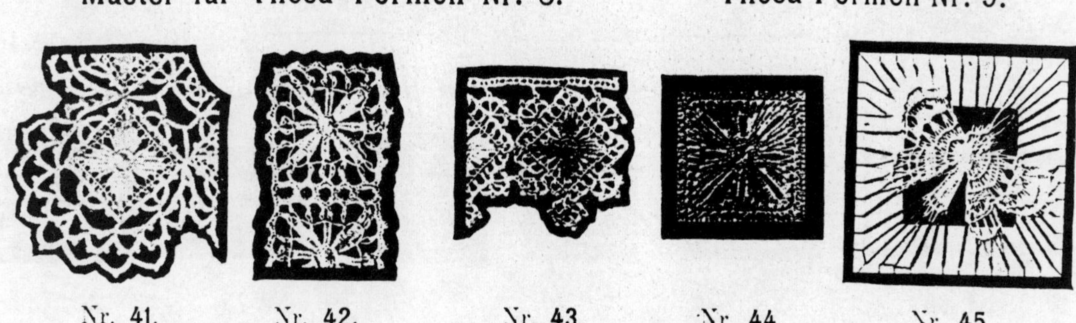

Nr. 41. Nr. 42. Nr. 43. Nr. 44. Nr. 45.

Muster für Thesa-Formen Nr. 9.

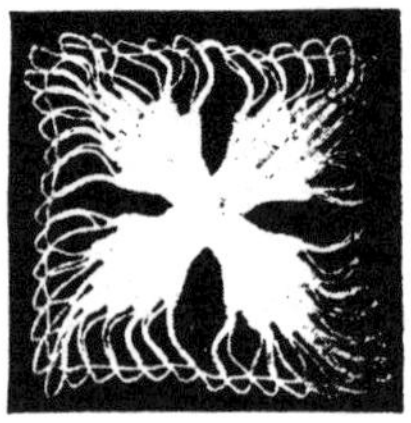

Nr. 46.  Nr. 47  Nr. 48.  Nr. 49.  Nr. 50.

Muster für Thesa-Formen Nr. 10.

Nr. 51. Nr. 53.  Nr. 54.  Nr. 52.

Nr. 55.  Nr. 56.  Nr. 57.  Nr. 58.

Nr. 59.  Nr. 60.  Nr. 61.  Nr. 62.

Muster für Thesa-Formen Nr. 11, 12, 13, 16 und 17.

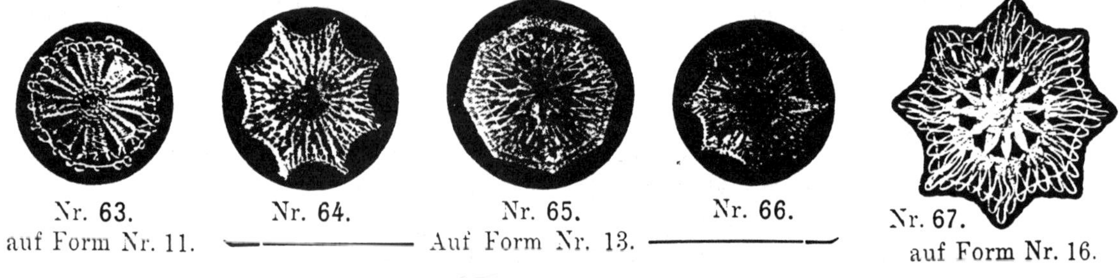

Nr. 63. auf Form Nr. 11. Nr. 64. Nr. 65. Nr. 66. Auf Form Nr. 13. Nr. 67. auf Form Nr. 16.

Muster für Thesa-Formen Nr. 14 und 15.

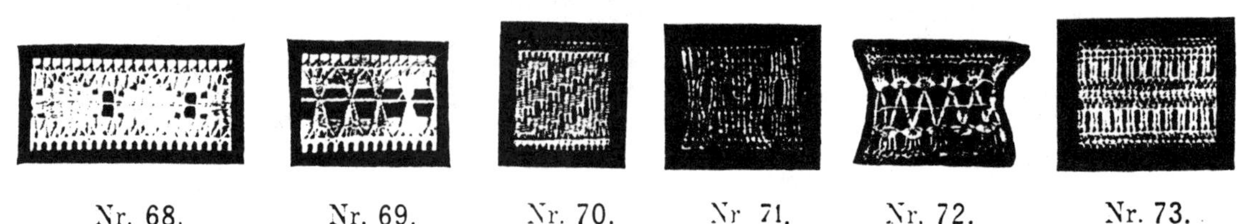

Nr. 68. Nr. 69. Nr. 70. Nr. 71. Nr. 72. Nr. 73.

Muster für Thesa-Formen Nr. 18.

Nr. 74.

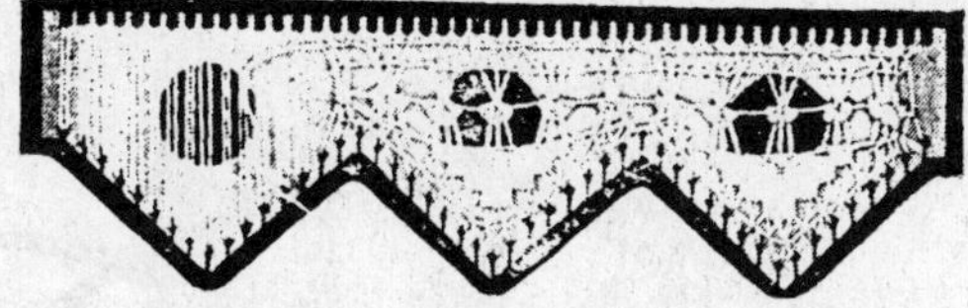
Nr. 75.

Muster für Thesa-Formen Nr. 19.

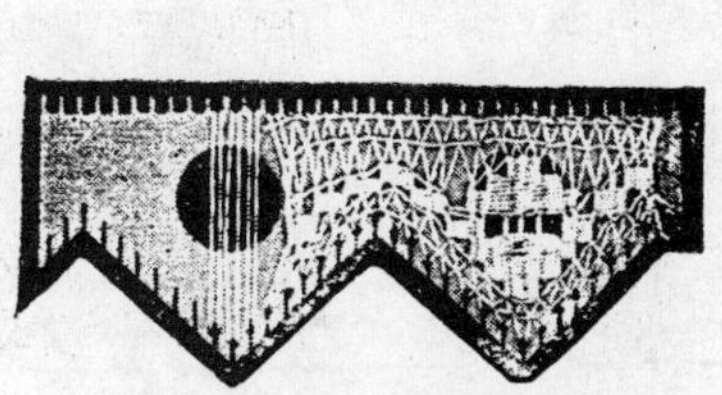
Nr. 76.

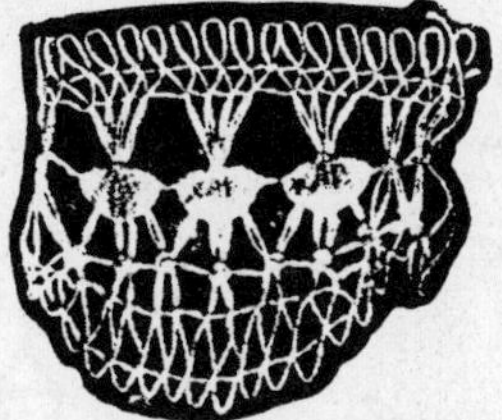
Nr. 77.

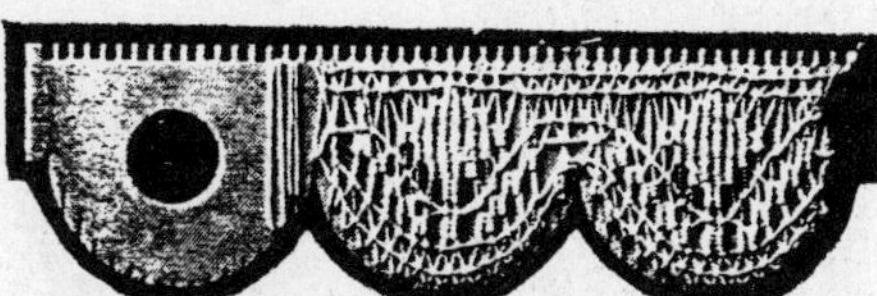
Nr. 78.

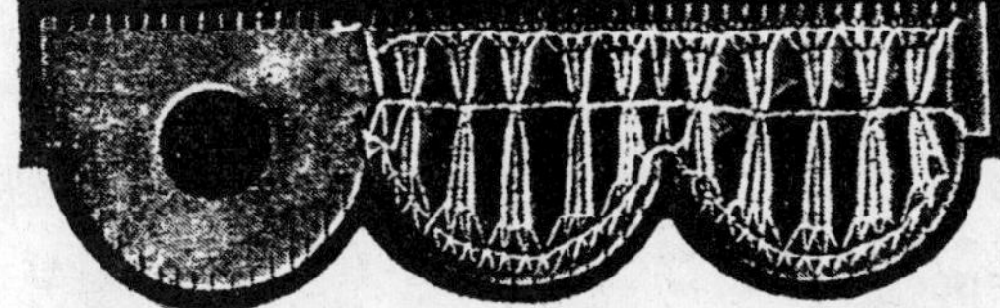
Nr. 79.

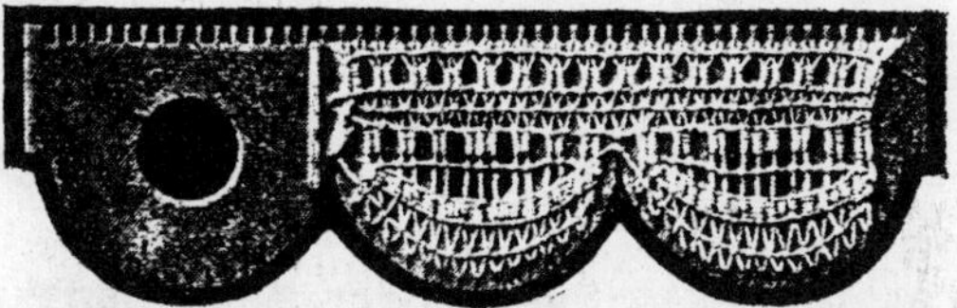
Nr. 80.

Muster für Thesa-Formen Nr. 21–26.

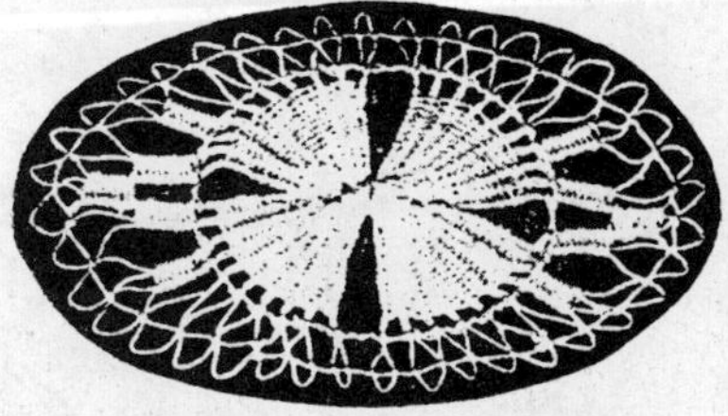
Nr. 81, für Form Nr. 20.

Nr. 82. für Form Nr. 21.

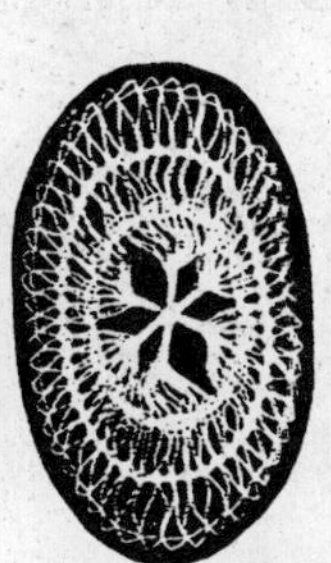
Nr. 83, für Form Nr. 22.

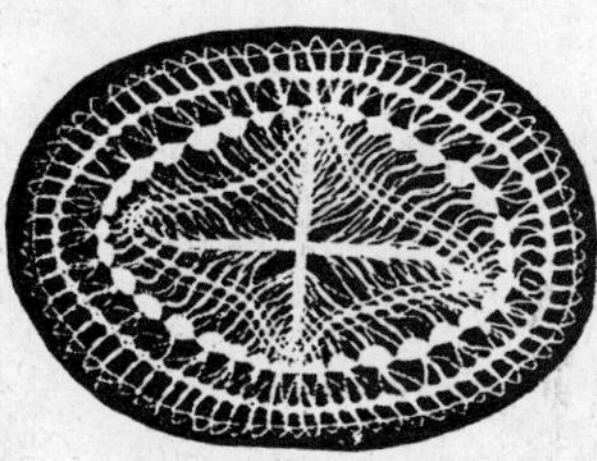
Nr. 84, für Form Nr. 23.

Nr. 85, für Form Nr. 24.

Nr. 86, für Form Nr. 24.

Nr. 87, für Form Nr. 24.

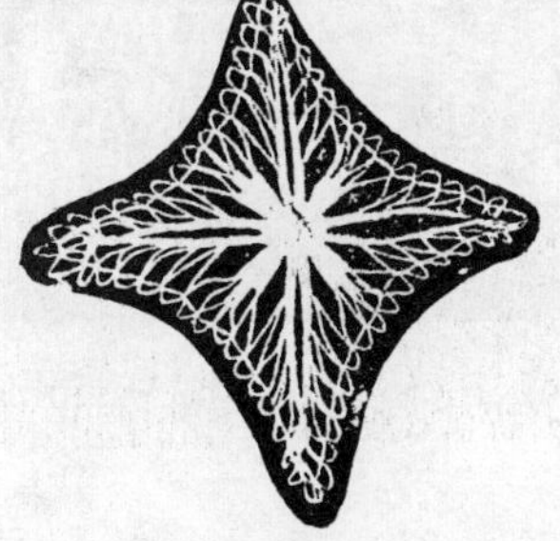
Nr. 88, für Form Nr. 25.

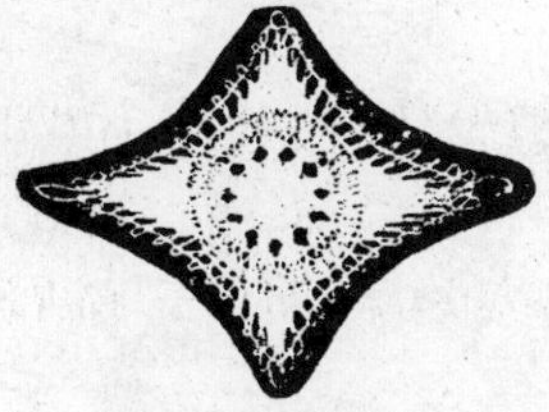
Nr. 89, für Form Nr. 26.

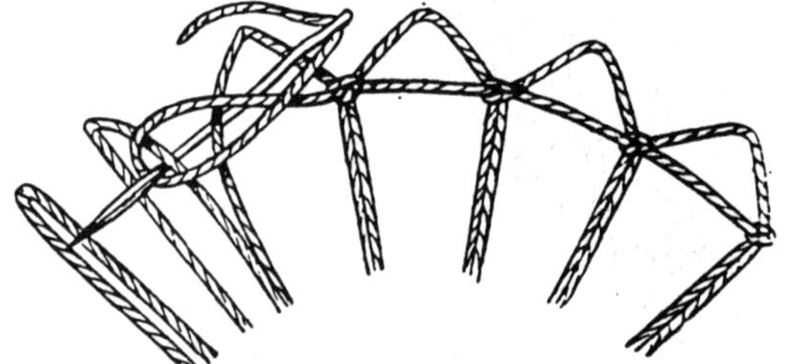

Abb. 10. Ausführung des **einfachen Bindeknotens** mit schrägem Kettenstich.

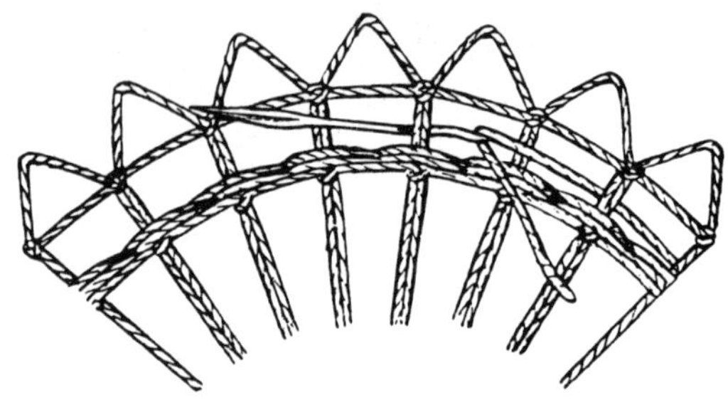

Abb. 12. **Weiter Stopfstich** als Füllung.

Abb. 11. Ausführung des **doppelten Bindeknotens.**

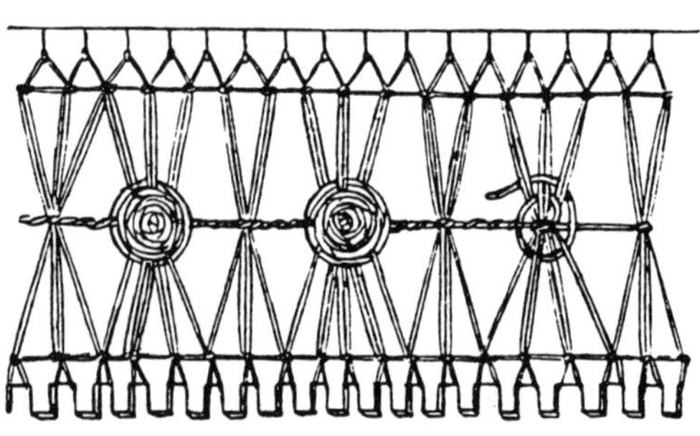

Abb. 15. Ausführung der **Zierspinne.**

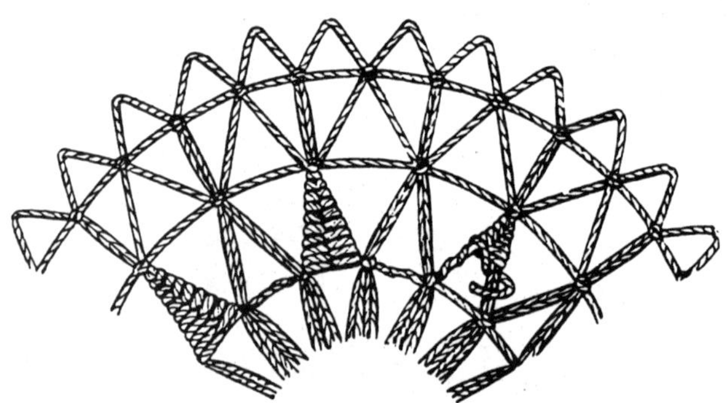

Abb. 13. Ausführung der **Stopfstichzäckchen.**

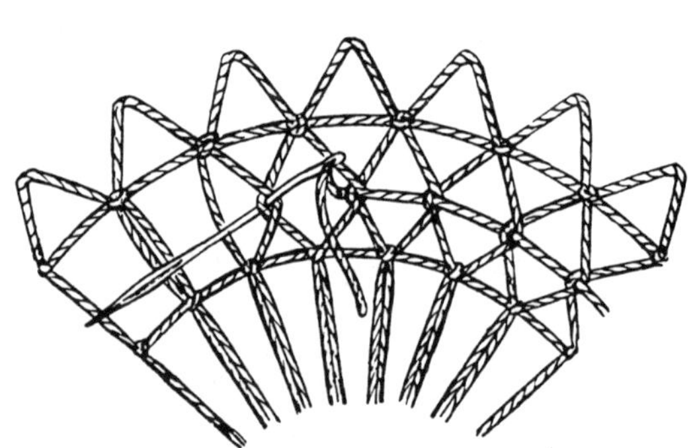

Abb. 17. Zweite Ausführung der **einfachen Ziernaht.**

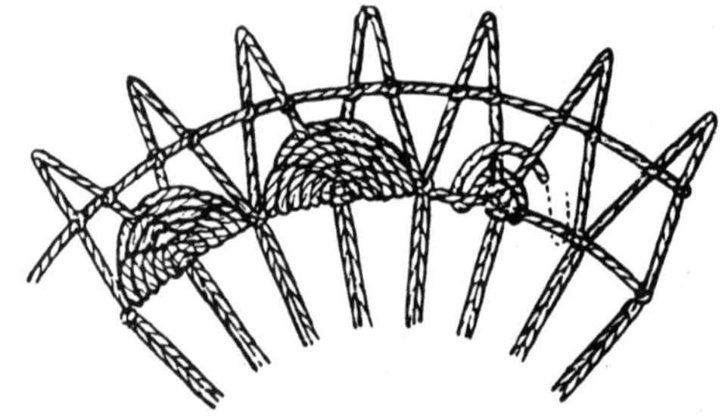

Abb. 14. Ausführung der **Stopfstichbogen.**

Abb. 18. Das Spannen zur Spitze u. Ausführung derselben.

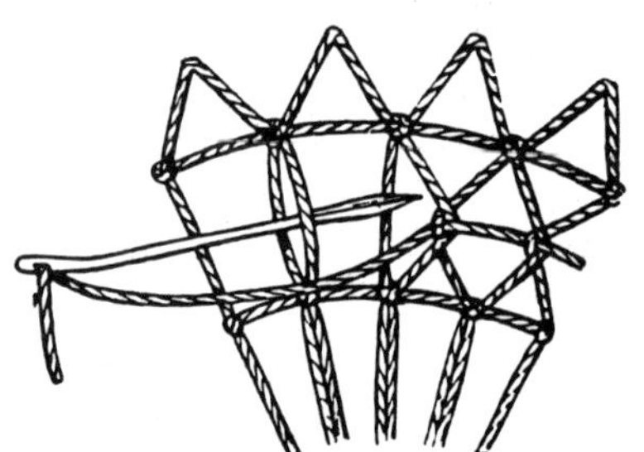

Abb. 16. Erste Ausführung der **einfachen Ziernaht.**

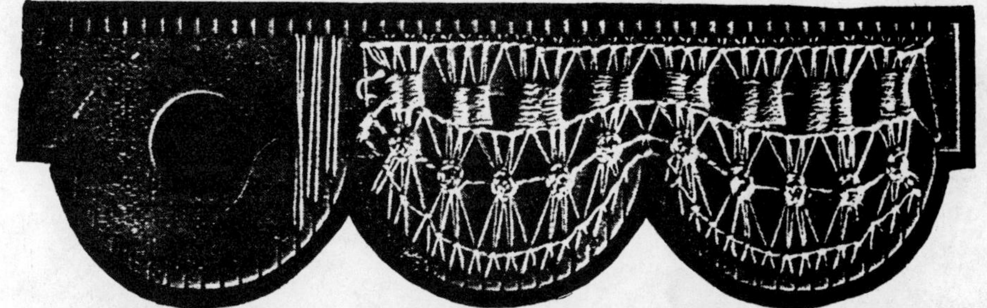

Abb. 19. Die Ausführung der **Bogenspitze.**

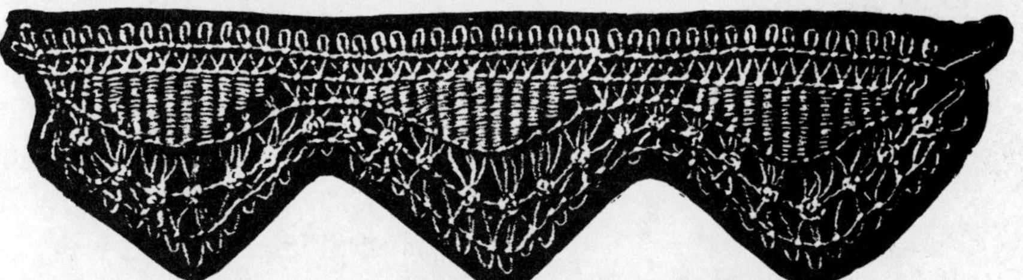

Abb. 20. **Fertige Zackenspitze.**

Abb. 21. Das **Fortführen des Spannfadens** nach dem Ablösen des fertigen Spitzenanfanges.

Abb. 22. **Kleid mit Thesa-Sternen und Hohlnaht-Verzierung.**

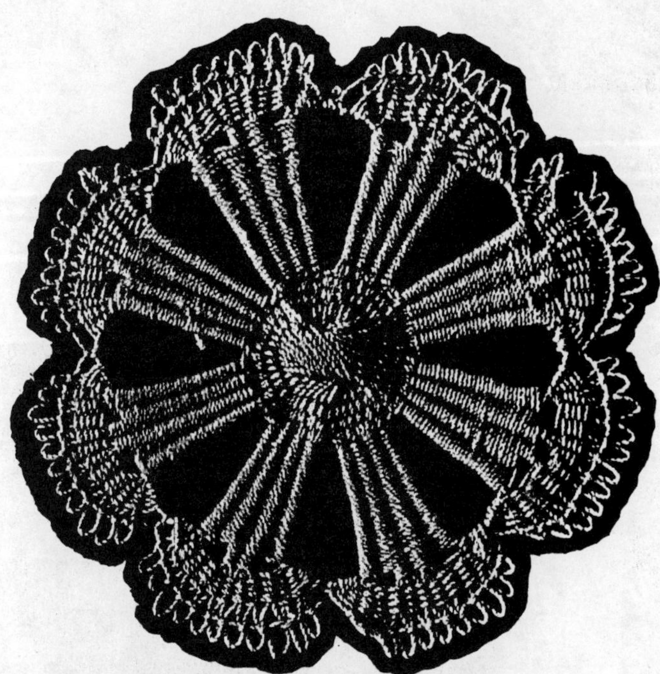

Abb. 23. **Naturgroße Ansicht des Sternes zum Kleid** Abb. 22 sowie zur Decke Seite 40, Abb. 120.

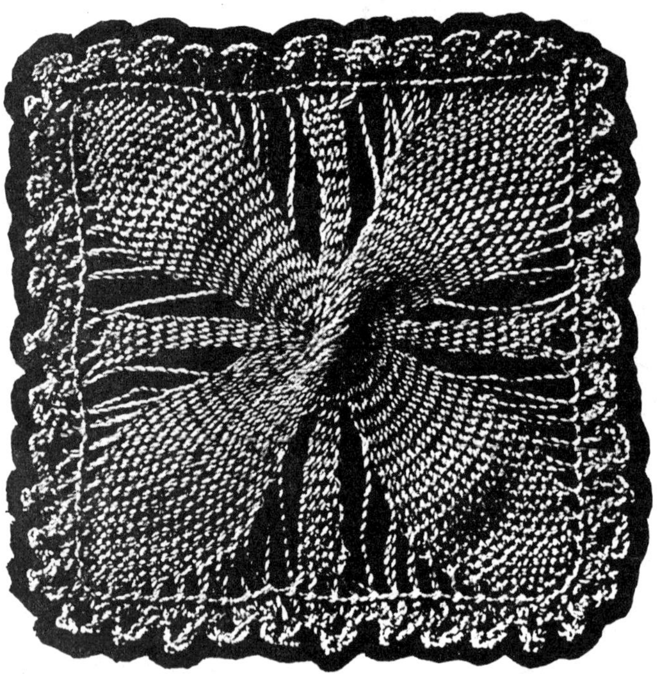

Abb. 26. Naturgroßes Quadrat zum Kleid Abb. 25.

Abb. 25. Kleid mit Thesa-Quadraten und Hohlnähten.
Naturgroße Einzelansicht Abb. 26.

Abb. 32. Elegantes Häubchen mit verschiedenen Sternen.

Abb. 33. Naturgroße Sterne f. Kinderkleidchen, Wäsche.

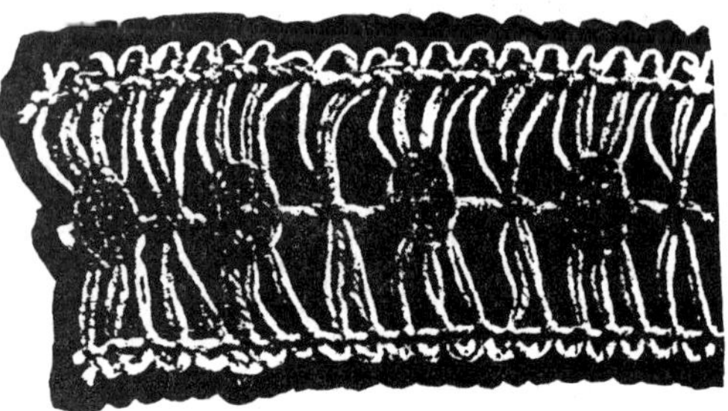

Abb. 35.

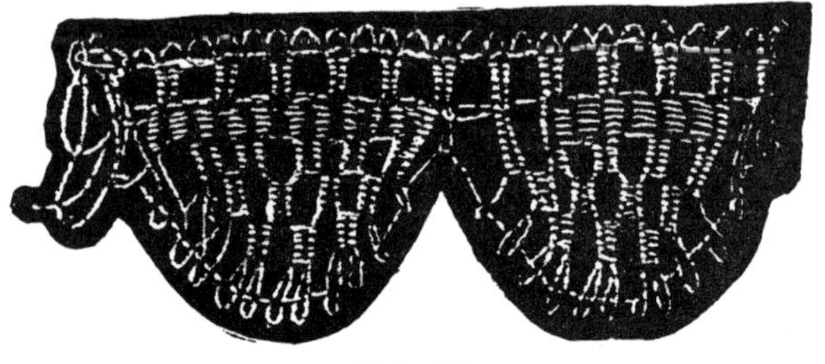

Abb. 35 a.

Abb. 30. **Naturgroßes Quadrat** zu Abb. 29.

Abb. 28.

Abb. 29.

Abb. 34.

Abb. 42.

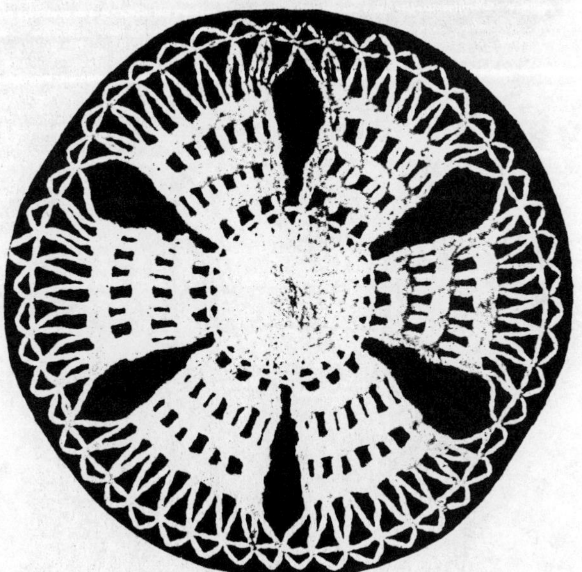

Abb. 31. **Thesa-Stern,** auf Form 3 gearbeitet.

Abb. 37. **Taghemd.**

Abb. 40.

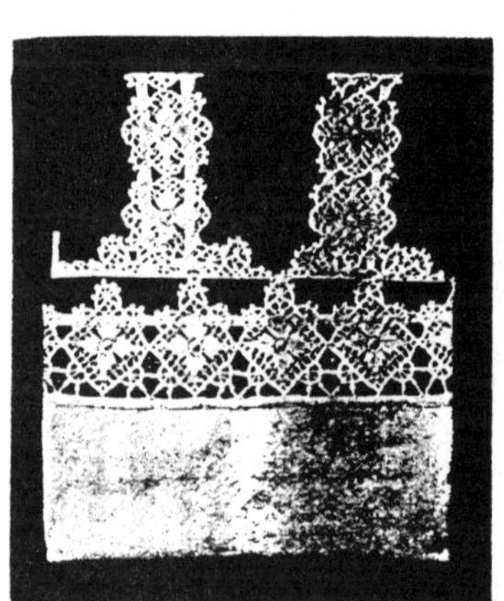

Abb. 36. **Taghemd.**

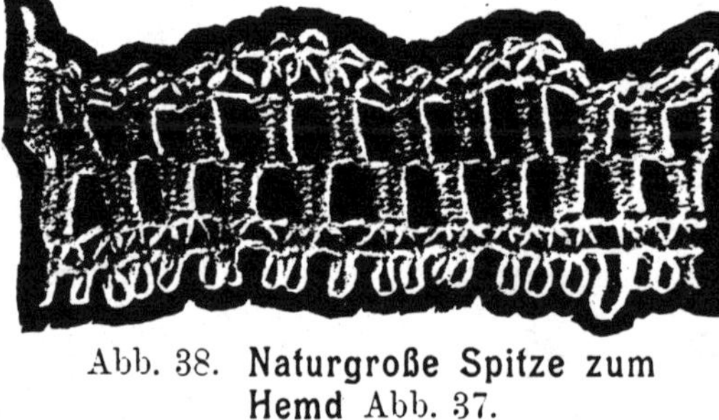

Abb. 38. **Naturgroße Spitze zum Hemd** Abb. 37.

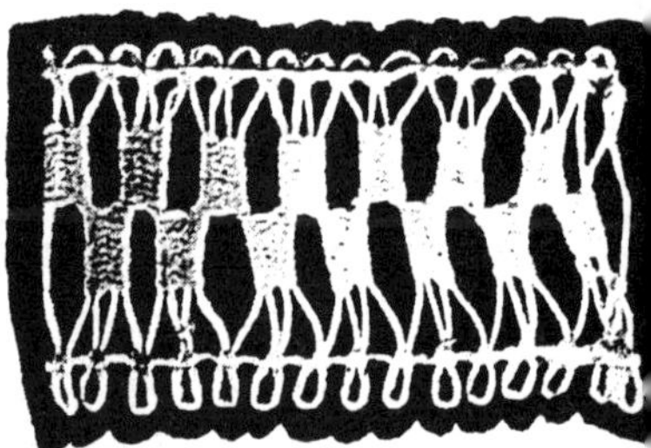

Abb. 39. **Naturgroßer Einsatz zum Hemd** Abb. 37.

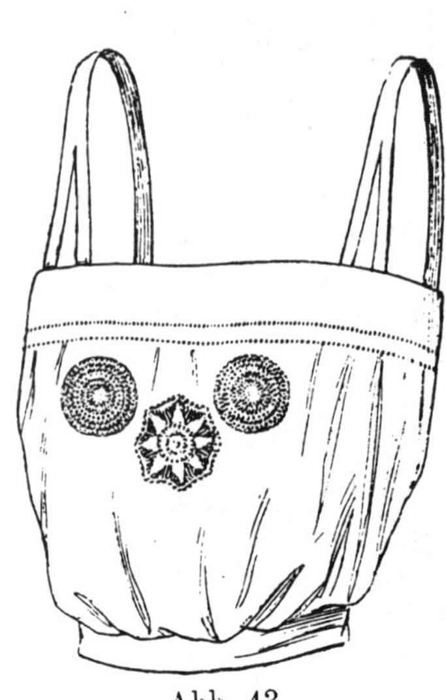

Abb. 43.

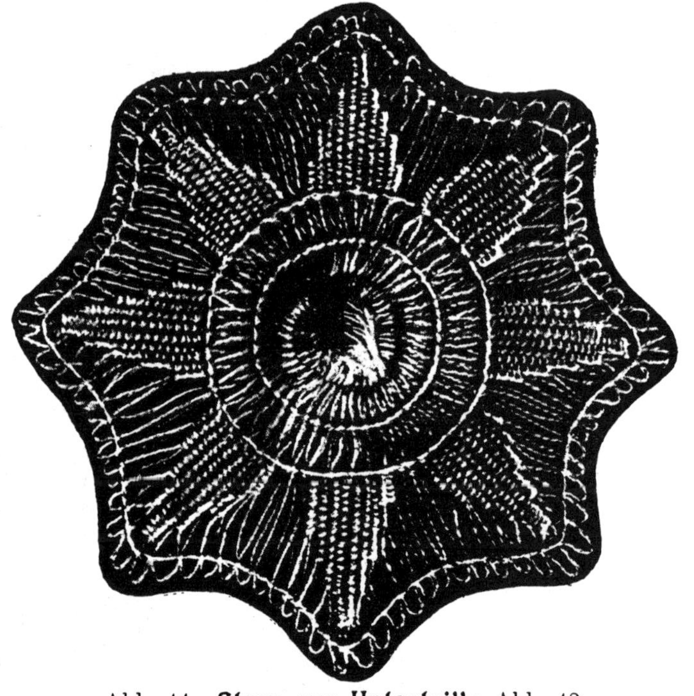

Abb. 44. **Stern zur Untertaille** Abb. 43, ausgeführt auf Form Nr. 17.

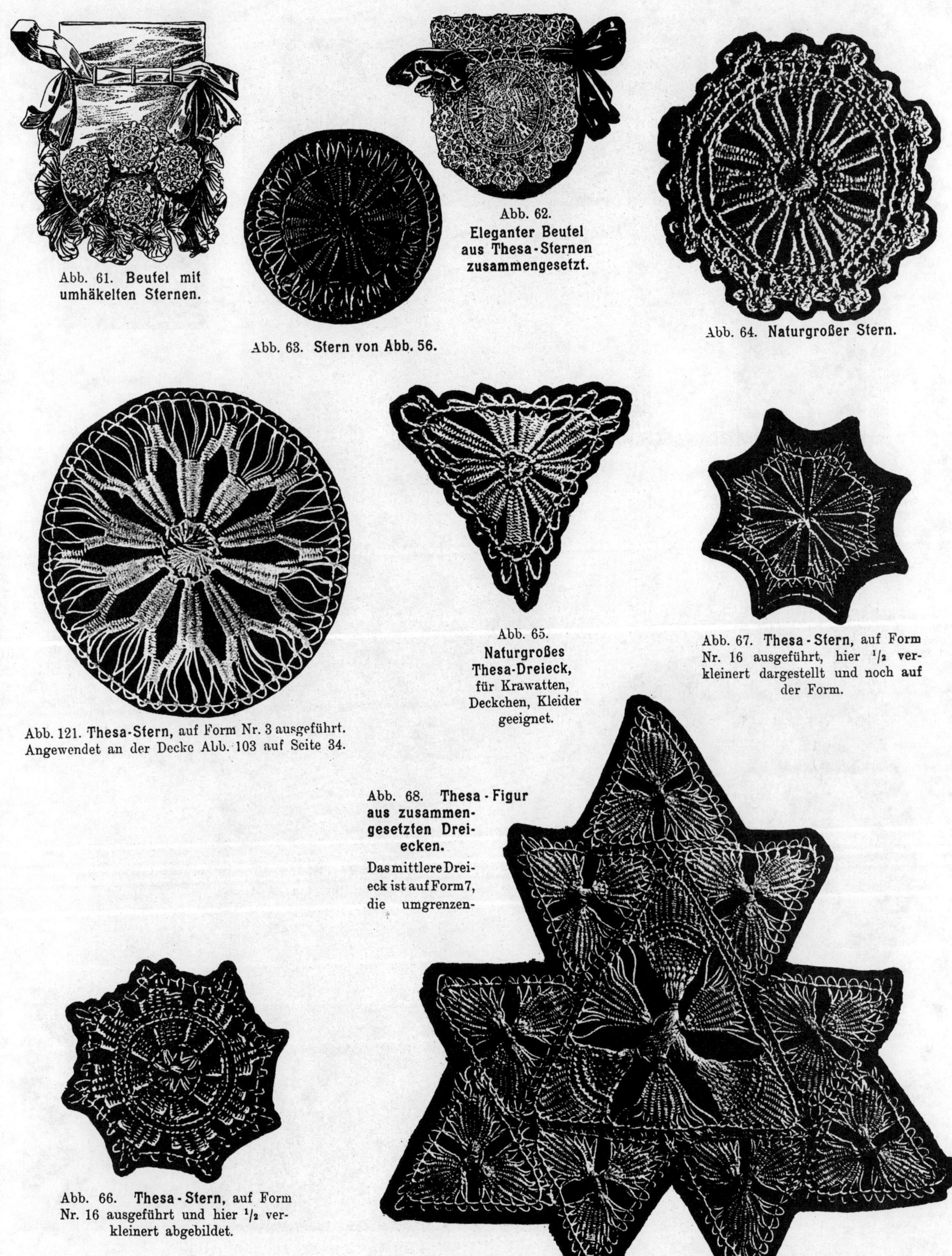

Abb. 61. **Beutel mit umhäkelten Sternen.**

Abb. 62. **Eleganter Beutel aus Thesa-Sternen zusammengesetzt.**

Abb. 63. **Stern von Abb. 56.**

Abb. 64. **Naturgroßer Stern.**

Abb. 121. **Thesa-Stern,** auf Form Nr. 3 ausgeführt. Angewendet an der Decke Abb. 103 auf Seite 34.

Abb. 65. **Naturgroßes Thesa-Dreieck,** für Krawatten, Deckchen, Kleider geeignet.

Abb. 67. **Thesa-Stern,** auf Form Nr. 16 ausgeführt, hier 1/2 verkleinert dargestellt und noch **auf** der Form.

Abb. 68. **Thesa-Figur aus zusammengesetzten Dreiecken.** Das mittlere Dreieck ist auf Form 7, die umgrenzen-

Abb. 66. **Thesa-Stern,** auf Form Nr. 16 ausgeführt und hier 1/2 verkleinert abgebildet.

Abb. 68.

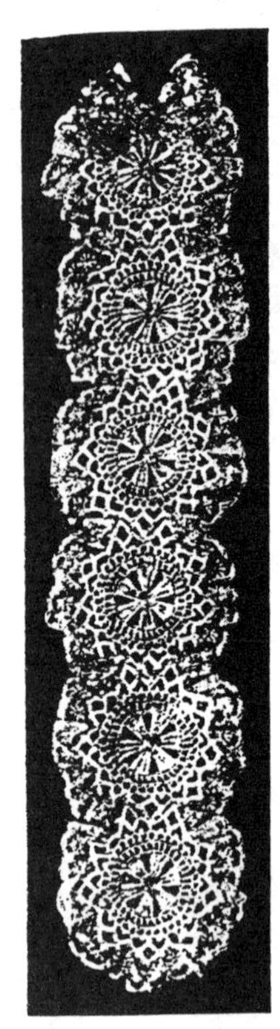

Abb. 47. **Mantelkragen mit gehäkeltem Grund.**

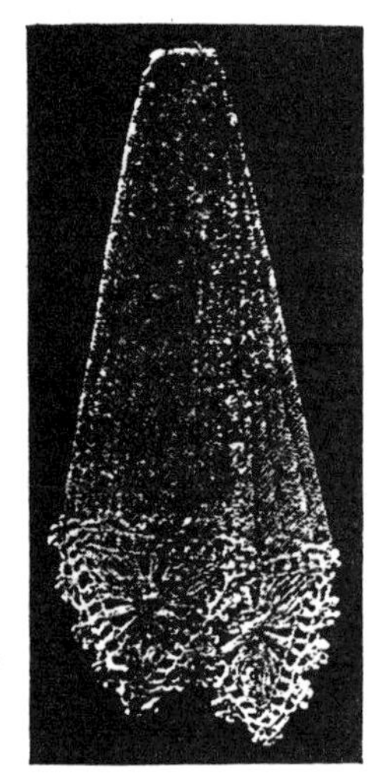

Abb. 49.
Tüllkrawatte.

Abb. 48.
Vorsteckstreifen.

Abb. 50. **Umhäkelter Stern** zu Abb. 47 und 48 sowie zum Kinderkleidchen Abb. 34 auf S. 14.

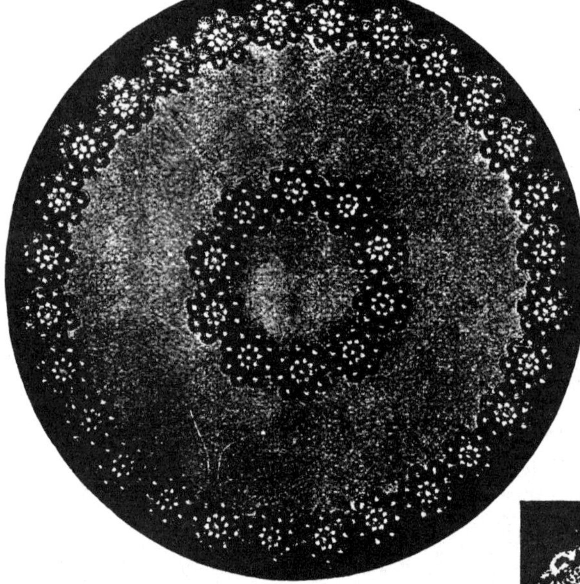

Abb. 92. **Runde Decke.**
Der größere Stern ist, wie ersichtlich, nach innen gebogt, was durch die Thesa-Form Nr. 16 erreicht wird.

Abb. 52. **Jackenkragen mit Thesa-Sternen.** Naturgroßer Stern Abb. 54.

Abb. 79. **Thesa-Quadrat,** auf Form Nr. 10 ausgeführt, zur Decke Abb. 78 passend.

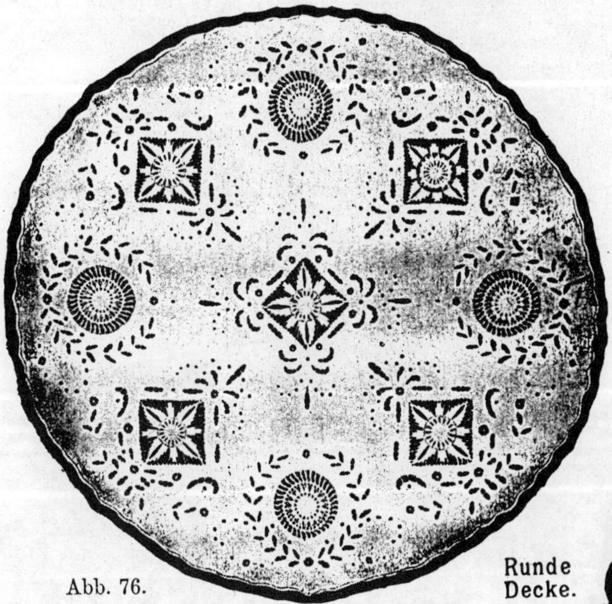

Abb. 76. **Runde Decke.**

Abb. 77. **Runde Decke.** Größe 80 cm.

Abb. 95. **Fensterpolster.**

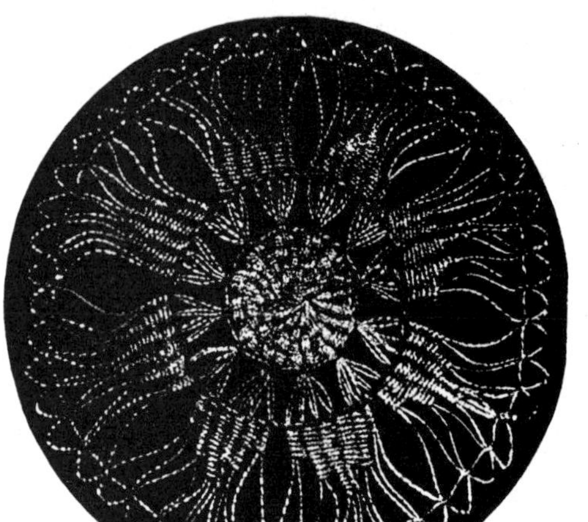

Abb. 112. **Thesa - Stern,** auf Form Nr. 3 ausgeführt und zur Decke Abb. 100 verwendet.

Abb. 78. **Runde Decke** mit Thesa-Figuren und Einsätzen und Lochstickerei.

Abb. 87. **Feine Leinendecke.** Größe 74 cm.

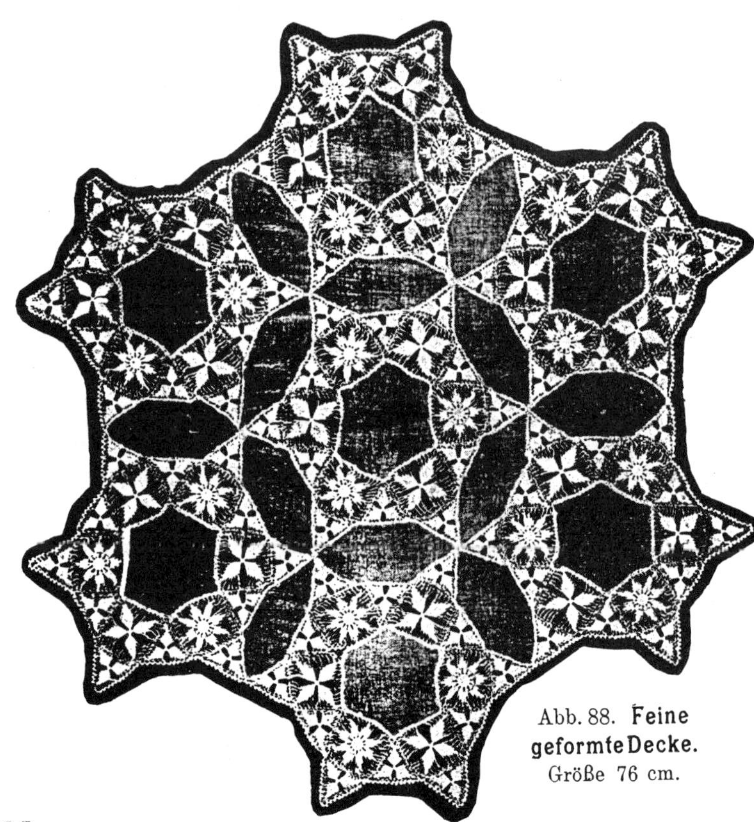

Abb. 88. **Feine geformte Decke.** Größe 76 cm.

Abb. 109. **Geschmackvoller Thesa-Stern** auf Form Nr. 17 auszuführen, für Kleider, Jabots u. Wäsche geeignet.

Abb. 99.

Abb. 100. **Runde Decke.**

Abb. 105. **Spitzendecke.**

Abb. 106. **Neuartige Decke.**

Abb. 103.

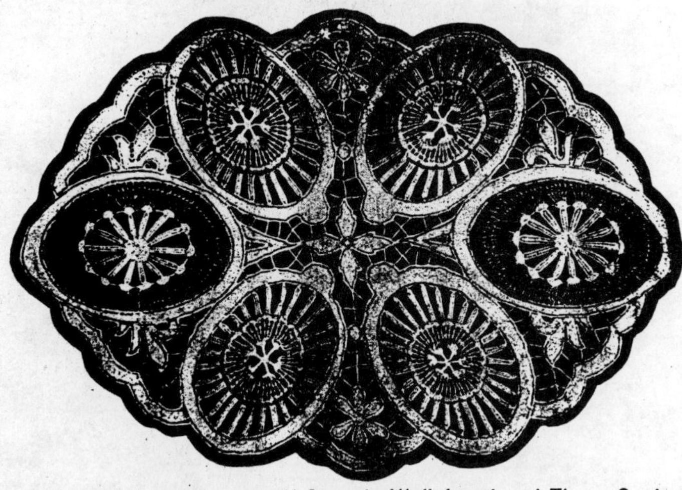

Abb. 107. **Ovale Decke mit Ausschnittstickerei und Thesa-Ovalen.**

Abb. 83.
Naturgroßer Stern
mit Häkelumrandg.

Abb. 70.

Abb. 69. **Tasche. Thesa - Quadrate aus Metallfäden und altgold. Tresse.**

Abb. 72.
Taschentuch mit drei versch. Sternen
Naturgr. Einzelheiten
Abb. 74 und 75.

Abb. 73. **Breit. Zackenkragen.**

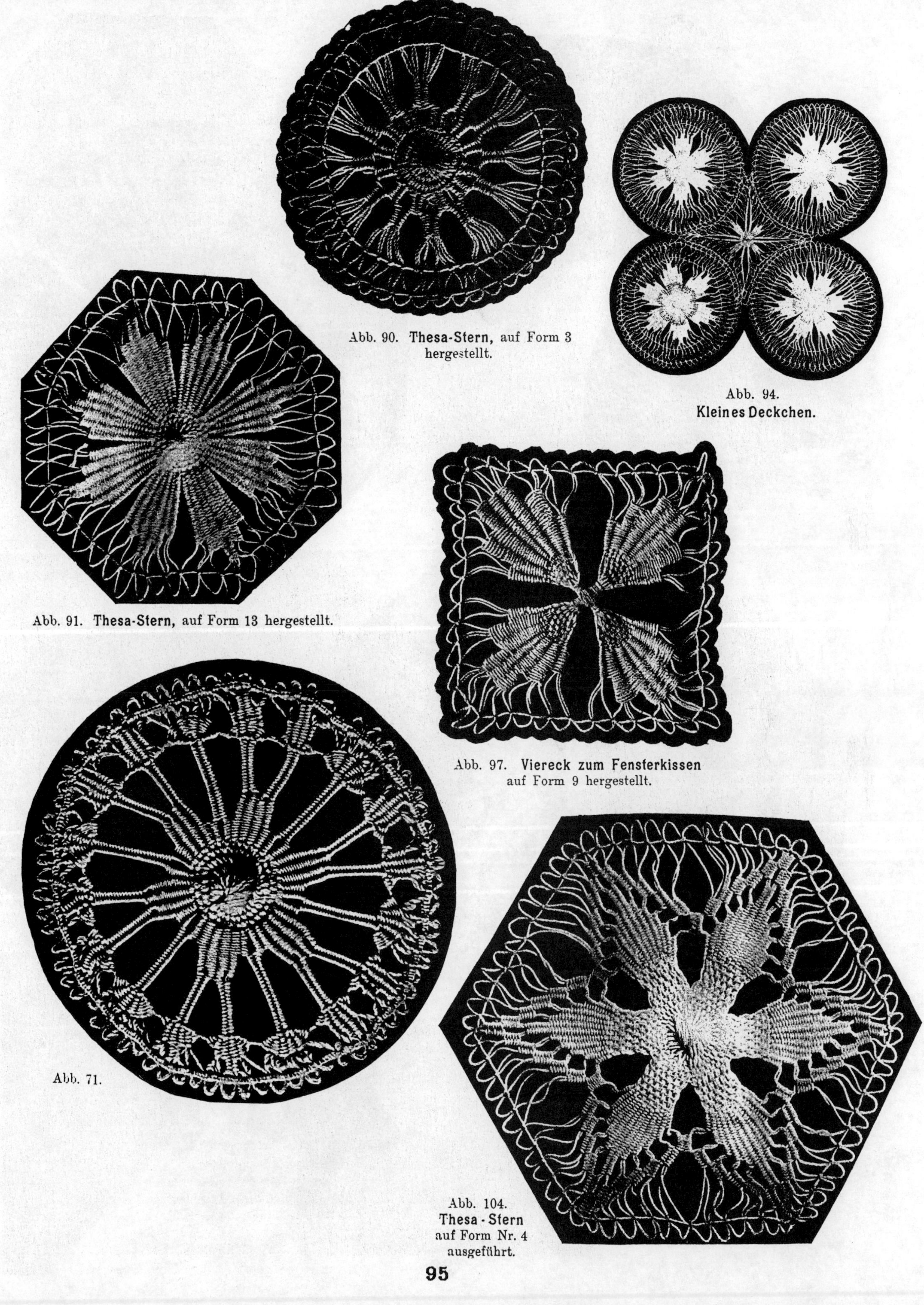

Abb. 90. **Thesa-Stern,** auf Form 3 hergestellt.

Abb. 94.
Kleines Deckchen.

Abb. 91. **Thesa-Stern,** auf Form 13 hergestellt.

Abb. 97. **Viereck zum Fensterkissen** auf Form 9 hergestellt.

Abb. 71.

Abb. 104.
Thesa - Stern
auf Form Nr. 4
ausgeführt.

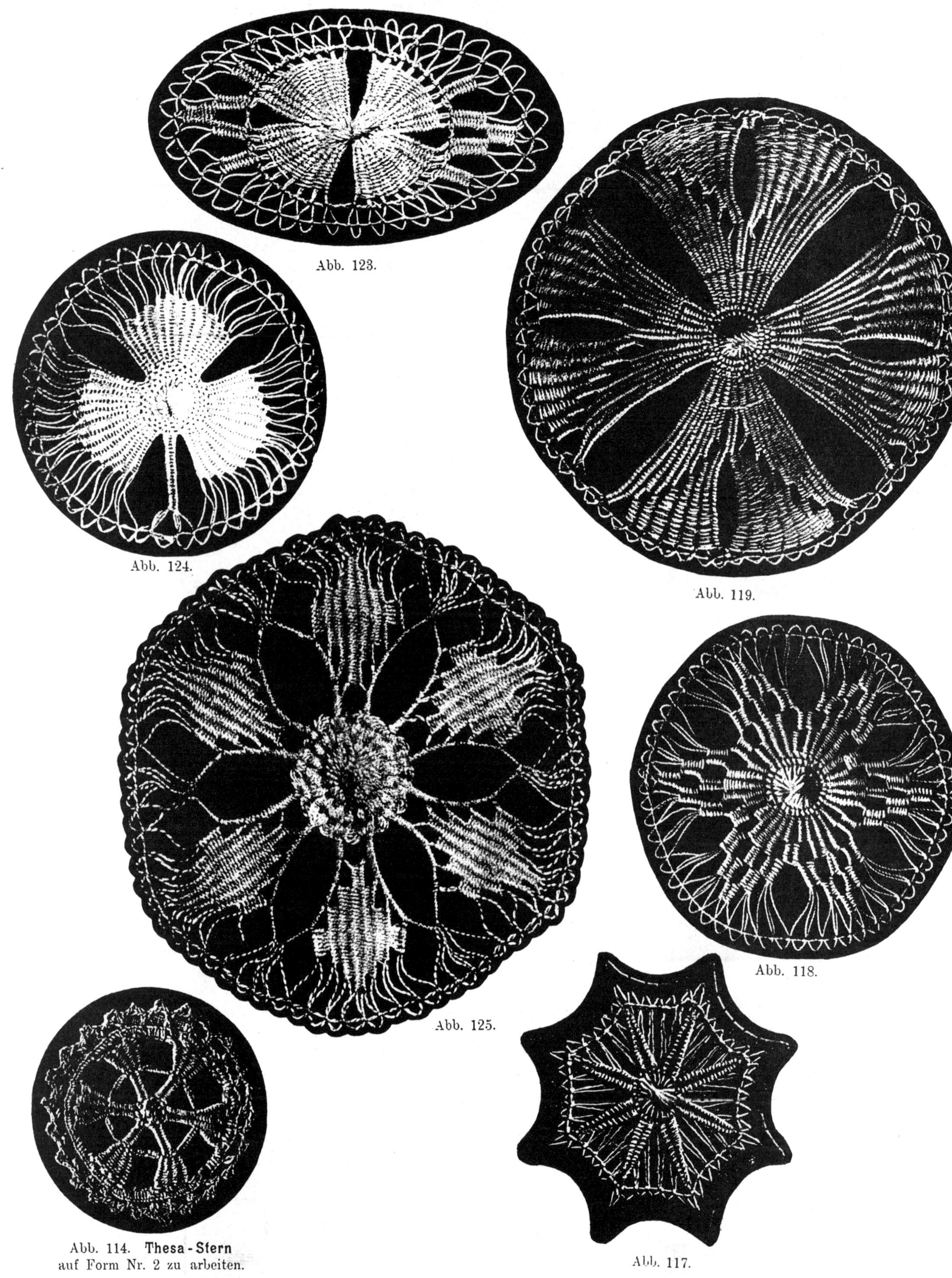

Abb. 123.

Abb. 124.

Abb. 119.

Abb. 118.

Abb. 125.

Abb. 114. **Thesa-Stern** auf Form Nr. 2 zu arbeiten.

Abb. 117.

Beauty & the Beast

The Story of a Fairy Tale

DAN STEVENS as the Beast and Emma Watson as Belle dance in the live-action Disney remake of the studio's classic 1991 animated feature.

MOVIESTORE/REX/SHUTTERSTOCK

EMMA WATSON in the new *Beauty and the Beast.*

Contents

FRONT COVER: Artwork © Mélanie Delon 2017
BACK COVER: Bettmann/Getty

MOVIESTORE/REX/SHUTTERSTOCK

LIFE

Beauty & the Beast

EDITOR AND WRITER J.I. Baker
DIRECTOR OF PHOTOGRAPHY Christina Lieberman
DESIGNER Sharon Okamoto
COPY CHIEF Parlan McGaw
COPY EDITOR Joel Van Liew
PICTURE EDITOR Rachel Hatch
WRITER-REPORTER Amy Lennard Goehner
PHOTO ASSISTANT Alessandra Bianco
DIRECTOR OF PHOTOGRAPHY EMERITA
Barbara Baker Burrows

TIME INC. BOOKS
PUBLISHER Margot Schupf
ASSOCIATE PUBLISHER Allison Devlin
VICE PRESIDENT, FINANCE Terri Lombardi
VICE PRESIDENT, MARKETING Jeremy Biloon
EXECUTIVE DIRECTOR, MARKETING SERVICES
Carol Pittard
DIRECTOR, BRAND MARKETING Jean Kennedy
SALES DIRECTOR Christi Crowley
ASSISTANT GENERAL COUNSEL Andrew Goldberg
ASSISTANT DIRECTOR, PRODUCTION
Susan Chodakiewicz
SENIOR MANAGER, CATEGORY MARKETING
Bryan Christian
BRAND MANAGER Katherine Barnet
ASSOCIATE PREPRESS MANAGER Alex Voznesenskiy
ASSOCIATE MANAGER FOR PROJECT MANAGEMENT
AND PRODUCTION Anna Riego

EDITORIAL DIRECTOR Kostya Kennedy
CREATIVE DIRECTOR Gary Stewart
DIRECTOR OF PHOTOGRAPHY Christina Lieberman
EDITORIAL OPERATIONS DIRECTOR Jamie Roth Major
SENIOR EDITOR Alyssa Smith
ASSOCIATE ART DIRECTOR Allie Adams
ASSISTANT ART DIRECTOR Anne-Michelle Gallero
COPY CHIEF Rina Bander
ASSISTANT MANAGING EDITOR Gina Scauzillo
ASSISTANT EDITOR Courtney Mifsud

TIME INC. PREMEDIA
Richard K. Prue (Director), Richard Shaffer (Production), Keith Aurelio, Kevin Hart, Rosalie Khan, Patricia Koh, Marco Lau, Brian Mai, Rudi Papiri, Clara Renauro

SPECIAL THANKS Brad Beatson, Melissa Frankenberry, Kristina Jutzi, Simon Keeble, Seniqua Koger, Kate Roncinske, Kristen Zwicker

Published by LIFE BOOKS, an imprint of Time Inc. Books
225 Liberty Street • New York, NY 10281

Vol. 17, No. 5 • March 3, 2017

We welcome your comments and suggestions about LIFE Books. Please write to us at:
LIFE Books, Attention: Book Editors
P.O. Box 62310, Tampa, FL 33662-2310

If you would like to order any of our hardcover Collector's Edition books, please call us at 800-327-6388, Monday through Friday, 7 a.m.–9 p.m. Central Time.

THE BEAUTY & THE BEAST, FOREVER

By Kostya Kennedy

The great love stories involve the overcoming of impediments—problems of distance and social strata, of familial bonds and rival lovers, of general circumstance. "Beauty and the Beast"? How is this for impediments: He lives in a massive, gloomy, fortified castle. She lives in a cottage in a sunny little village near a bookshop. He wants to keep her father locked up in a cell. She does not want her father to be kept locked up in a cell. He is a two-legged warthog, perhaps, or a wolfman, or some other improbable species. She is a human being.

And yet...

Love of course—and here's a spoiler alert for cave dwellers—triumphs over all in "Beauty and the Beast." But the story's exceptional endurance in popular culture—a tale as old as time, as Disney's singing teapot reminds us—rests not in a simple Hallmark message but in its layers of complexity, in the psychological wires it trips. The core suggestion that each of us, no matter how hideous or beastly we may appear or feel ourselves to be, can both give and receive love is powerful enough to propel a good yarn. Belle's disappointment when the once fearsome Beast is transformed into a handsome prince is, not unlike Cinderella's forgiving of her depraved stepsisters, a mark of humanity at its most encouraging. "Where is my Beast?" she asks the prince indignantly. Belle doesn't love the new guy *because* of the haircut and the jawline but in spite of them.

Beauty, though, runs deeper. There's a whiff of Stockholm syndrome in the story (not only Belle's father, but also Belle herself is essentially imprisoned by the Beast). There's a trace of the Electra complex. (Belle is her dear old dad's life mate; in true fairy tale fashion there's no mother in the picture.) There is a hint, too, of Adam and Eve, though here it is a plucked rose rather than a plucked apple that gets the action rolling.

Regardless of exactly when and where the story of "Beauty and the Beast" first arose (those plausible historical underpinnings are splendidly traced in the pages ahead) the genesis of our affection for it clearly comes from within, true in 2017 as in 1917 as in 1617. And in the sprawling, centuries-old archive of fairy tales—"Snow White" and "The Princess Bride," "The Frog Prince" and "The Ugly Duckling," "Aladdin" and "Tom Thumb"—it may be that "Beauty and the Beast," replete with a magic spell, a mystery, and, lately, an impertinent dancing candelabra, is the richest tale of them all.

BEAUTY AND THE BEAST
ILLUSRATION
BY
Walter Crane

The Beast's Beginnings

A story from ancient Rome becomes a modern classic in courtly France

Once upon a time, a merchant who had lost his fortune traveled overseas in search of new opportunities. Before he left home, he asked his three beautiful daughters what they wanted him to bring back. Two asked for treasure, but the third—so beautiful that she was called Beauty—asked for a simple rose.

On his return journey, the merchant was shipwrecked on an island, where he stayed overnight in a mysterious castle owned by a fearsome man-beast. Remembering Beauty's request, he picked a rose from the castle arbor—only to be interrupted by the creature. Angry at the merchant's theft of his beloved flower, the Beast demanded that he pay for it with either his life or the gift of one of his daughters.

When Beauty heard of this ultimatum, she decided—against her father's wishes—to sacrifice herself. She ended up at the castle, where every night, over dinner, the Beast asked her if she would marry him. Every night she said no. But despite the Beast's fearsome aspect, Beauty came to understand that he had a warm and loving heart.

One night, gazing in her magic mirror, Beauty discovered that her father was gravely ill, so she begged the Beast to let her return home. He agreed—on the condition that she return within a week. Otherwise, he said, he would die.

Hearing this story, Beauty's ever-jealous sisters conspired to delay Beauty, and when she finally returned to the castle the Beast was near

THE METROPOLITAN MUSEUM OF ART/ART RESOURCE, NY

THIS 1901 WOOD engraving, by English artist Walter Crane (whose 1877 illustration is seen on page 5), shows the dying Beast as a humanoid boar—just one of many incarnations he has taken over the years.

ERICH LESSING/ART RESOURCE, NY

LAUDATE PUERI DOMINUM.

LAUDATE NOMEN DOMINI.

ILLUSTRATED LONDON NEWS LTD/MARY EVANS

SOME HAVE CALLED Petrus Gonsalvus, opposite, the historical inspiration for the modern "Beauty and the Beast" story—even though the source of the tale itself, an iteration of the archetypal animal bridegroom legend, is lost in prehistory. Above: Two of Gonsalvus's children who, like him, suffered from hypertrichosis, the excessive growth of body hair.

death. Bereft, Beauty told him that she loved him, causing the Beast to morph into a handsome prince, who revealed that he had been cursed to live as an animal until a young virgin fell in love with him.

Of course, they both lived happily ever after.

In essence, this is the version of "Beauty and the Beast" that we now know and love, but it is just one of many. Over the years, the Beast has been represented as a frog, a ram, a bear, and a pig. He may even have been based on a living person.

BORN AROUND 1550 IN TENERIFE, Spain, Petrus Gonsalvus suffered from a rare disorder known as hypertrichosis (also known as werewolf syndrome or Ambras syndrome) that caused his entire body to be covered in hair. Dubbed "the man of the woods" by naturalist and physician Ulisse Aldrovandi, Gonsalvus was the first recorded case of the disorder.

Despite his condition, Gonsalvus became a member of the court of Henry II of France, eventually marrying, and siring several children (some of whom inherited the disorder). In the late 1500s, an anonymous German artist painted a series of portraits of Gonsalvus, collectively titled "Der Rauchmann zu München"

CONTINUED ON PAGE 13

SYLVAIN SONNET/GETTY

THE BEAST'S CASTLE in Disney's animated film was modeled after Château de Chambord, a 16th-century hunting lodge in Loir-et-Cher, France, according to *Travel & Leisure*. It has 426 rooms, 282 chimneys, and 77 staircases.

HAMMERSMITH AND FULHAM COUNCIL, LONDON/BRIDGEMAN IMAGES

BRIDGEMAN IMAGES

CONTINUED FROM PAGE 9

(literally meaning "The Smoke Man of Munich"). One of these is featured in the Chamber of Art and Curiosities in Ambras Castle, Austria.

But the purely literary source of "Beauty and the Beast" was probably *The Golden Ass,* a novel by Apuleius written in the 2nd century—the only ancient Roman text to survive in its entirety. Part of the book is devoted to the story of Cupid and Psyche, which goes something like this:

Once upon a time there lived a king with three daughters. Though they were all beautiful, the youngest, Psyche, was so stunning that she made Venus, the goddess of love, jealous. So Venus asked her son, Cupid, to use one of his arrows to force the girl to fall in love with a monster.

Soon smitten with Psyche himself, Cupid lured her to a mysterious castle without betraying his identity. There, every night, he joined the young girl in their dark bedroom, calling himself her husband. But she was left alone during the day, and she was lonely, so she convinced her so-called husband to let her sisters visit. Jealous of Psyche's life in the luxurious castle, they decided to destroy her marriage by convincing

CONTINUED ON PAGE 16

A 1867 PAINTING by the Pre-Raphaelite artist Edward Burne-Jones, *Cupid Delivering Psyche*, is shown at left, reflecting the first known literary iteration of "Beauty and the Beast." Above: One of many scenes from Apuleius's *The Golden Ass* that were painted by Vincenzo Tamagni around 1530.

MOVIESTORE/REX/SHUTTERSTOCK

DAN STEVENS as the Beast and Emma Watson as Belle in the 2017 Disney remake of the studio's classic 1991 animated feature. The fairy tale's passive heroine was made more modern and active in the '91 version, qualities that were amplified even further in the remake. "We tried to tweak things to make [her] more proactive . . . and a bit more in charge of—and in control of—her own destiny," Watson told *Entertainment Weekly*.

CONTINUED FROM PAGE 13

Psyche that her mysterious husband was, in fact, a monster.

One night, determined to discover the truth, Psyche carried a lamp into the pitch-black room where her husband slept. When she shined it on him, she saw not a monster but the beautiful boy Cupid, who eventually convinced Zeus, the most powerful of all the gods, to make Psyche an immortal.

Though the tale itself may be 4,000 years old, according to researchers at Durham University, this is the earliest known version. "We certainly have no way of finding out what was the particular psychological state of the unknown and unknowable person who invented the story," folklore scholar Stith Thompson once said. What's certain is that the story reflects an ancient tradition of so-called animal bridegroom stories, about beautiful women who marry beasts.

In *Beauty and the Beast: Tales from Around the World,* Heidi Anne Heiner identifies two versions of "Cupid and Psyche," 23 versions of "Beauty and the Beast," and 162 versions of the animal bridegroom story, which—from *The Golden Ass* on—have significantly influenced mainstream literature.

Shakespeare, for one, used the idea to comic effect in *A Midsummer Night's Dream,* which he wrote in the 1590s. In it, Robin Goodfellow (Puck) magically causes Titania, the

PRINCESS VASILISA *and the Giant Lobster* (a painting by Filipp Andreyevich Malyavin, one of the leading Russian artists of the early 20th century) reflects an element of the classic Slavic folktale about the mythical Firebird.

HIP/ART RESOURCE, NY

Ph Maliavine

CCI/REX/SHUTTERSTOCK

HIP/ART RESOURCE, NY

Queen of the Fairies, to fall in love with Bottom, a lowly weaver, who has been magically transformed—at least in part—into a donkey. "My mistress with a monster is in love," says Puck.

But the animal bridegroom is just one of many enduring fairy-tale categories. "The fairy tale was first a simple, imaginative oral tale that contained magical and miraculous elements and was related to the belief systems, values, rites, and experiences of pagan peoples," Jack Zipes, professor emeritus at the University of Minnesota, tells LIFE. "Also known as the wonder or magic tale, it underwent numerous transformations before the innovation of print led to the production of fixed texts. They were like predigital memes transformed by common nonliterate people and by upper-class literate people."

Nearly every culture in the world has developed oral wonder tales, Zipes adds. "They existed in Africa and Asia long before they were developed in Europe," he says. "There are hundreds of types that have been disseminated throughout the world and take on different cultural meanings even though there are similarities in form, structure, and substance. For instance, the treatment of women will always be different in individual countries

CONTINUED ON PAGE 23

AN ILLUSTRATION for the Hungarian fairy tale "The Stake" by Ernö Dezsö, circa 1911, at left. Opposite: A 1923 illustration for "The Garden of Paradise," published in 1839 by Hans Christian Andersen, shows a prince riding the east wind to the titular garden. The story ends with the prince facing a personified death, who says, "I shall lay him in a black coffin, place it on my head, and fly away with it beyond the stars." Sweet dreams, children.

EVERETT

THE OPULENT and excessive 1935 Warner Bros. film of *A Midsummer Night's Dream* starred James Cagney as Bottom, Mickey Rooney as Puck, and newcomer Olivia de Havilland as Hermia. Here, Titania (Anita Louise) falls in love with Cagney's beastly Bottom while both are under magic spells. "Come, sit thee down upon this flowery bed," she says, "While I thy amiable cheeks do coy."

A. Guillon.

DEAGOSTINI/GETTY

THE MARSDEN ARCHIVE/ALAMY

CONTINUED FROM PAGE 18

despite the fact that the tale type is universally recognizable."

Unlike most fairy tales, "Beauty and the Beast" as we know it has verifiable literary—as opposed to oral—origins. In 1740, Madame Gabrielle-Suzanne de Villeneuve published her version in *La Jeune Amériquaine et les contes marins* (*The Young American Girl and the Marine Tales*). She had been inspired by stories she had heard in French salons—chief among them those of Charles Perrault, who lived and wrote in the 1600s. Called the father of the fairy tale, Perrault almost single-handedly defined such ancient stories as "Cinderella," "Little Red Riding Hood," and "Bluebeard."

Another likely influence was "The Pig King" by Gianfrancesco Straparola, who in the 1500s published his literary versions of oral tales in *The Pleasant Nights*. Very much unlike the children's stories we know now, they were violent and risqué. When the filthy Pig King's sexual advances are rejected by his first two wives, for instance, he simply kills them. Knowing that she, too, will die if she rejects him, the Pig King's third wife agrees to have sex with him—and is pleasantly surprised. In fact, she emerges "all defiled with mud... and looking pleased and contented."

AN ILLUSTRATION for "Bluebeard" by Adolphe Guillon, from a 19th-century Parisian edition of Charles Perrault's tales, is shown opposite. The story is often thought to reflect the life of Gilles de Rais, a child murderer and friend of Joan of Arc. Above: Champtocé, the castle in Anjou, France, where de Rais was born.

CCI/REX/SHUTTERSTOCK

MARY EVANS

So who needs a handsome prince?

But Villeneuve's greatest influence was probably the writer Madame Marie-Catherine d'Aulnoy, who coined the term *fairy tale* in her 1697 collection, *Les Contes des Fées* (*Tales of the Fairies*).

Here's how her story "The Ram" begins:

Once upon a time, when fairies were alive, there lived a king who had three daughters. They were beautiful, young, and good, but the youngest, Merveilleuse, was the loveliest and most beloved of all.

In the story, Merveilleuse goes to live with the princely Ram, who dies after she leaves him—"stretched on the pavement," d'Aulnoy writes, "all the life gone out of him!" Merveilleuse then runs to him, "weeping and groaning for she knew her delay had caused the death of the royal ram. In her despair, she was

CONTINUED ON PAGE 29

THE HERO OF yet another animal bridegroom tale, "The Frog King," is shown at left with the story's princess in a 1900 Hungarian postcard. Above: The Beast takes the form of a benevolent royal ram in this 1819 image from an influential early version of the story by Madame Marie-Catherine d'Aulnoy.

PETER MOUNTAIN/WALT DISNEY STUDIOS MOTION PICTURES/EVERETT

LILLA CRAWFORD played Little Red Riding Hood in *Into the Woods*, the 2014 Disney film of the Tony Award-winning 1987 Stephen Sondheim musical. (Johnny Depp played the Wolf.) The film intertwines several tales of the Brothers Grimm and Charles Perrault in the story of a childless baker and his wife who want to start a family.

ERICH LESSING/ART RESOURCE, NY

GILLES TARGAT/PHOTO12/POLARIS

CONTINUED FROM PAGE 25

likely to die herself."

Beauty and her Beast would not live happily ever after until 1757, when Jeanne-Marie Leprince de Beaumont published her revision of Villeneuve's tale in *Le Magasin des Enfants* (*The Children's Magazine*). Even more than Villeneuve, Beaumont brought a courtly, urban, Gallic influence to the tale, creating the version that is best known today.

"'Beauty and the Beast' reflects... an emerging bourgeoisie in prerevolutionary France, one that functions in a moral, social, and financial economy very different from that of feudal time," according to Maria Tatar, a professor of Germanic languages and literatures at Harvard University. It also reflects women's anxiety about the arranged marriages that were common at the time, she added.

But Villeneuve and Beaumont's world would collapse forever in 1789, when the French Revolution led to the Napoleonic Wars. Against this backdrop, two German scholars began collecting folktales and fairy tales, trying to preserve an aspect of their threatened culture.

They were called the Brothers Grimm.

THE HALL OF MIRRORS at the Palace of Versailles in France, opposite, reflects the courtly France where the modern version of "Beauty and the Beast" first took shape. But that world vanished with the French Revolution, after which Queen Marie-Antoinette was executed on October 16, 1793, shown in the painting above.

The Brothers Grimm

Two German siblings turn beautiful and beastly folklore into stories for kids

In the first decade of the 19th century, as students at the University of Marburg in the German principality of Hesse, brothers Jacob and Wilhelm Grimm were focusing on what they believed to be their lives' work—the creation of a German dictionary—when they began collecting local folklore (*Märchen*) as a favor to a friend. Trying to preserve distinctly German oral traditions at a time of increasing nationalism, the brothers took up residence in the city of Kassel, also in Hesse, and started to gather stories from area residents. Soon they amassed 49 traditional tales representing narratives that had been told and retold over centuries—in taverns, spinning rooms, and nurseries.

Many of these stories—and others that came later—reflect the animal bridegroom theme that inspired "Beauty and the Beast." They included "The Three Feathers," in which a simpleton encounters a toad who transforms into a beautiful young woman; "The Poor Miller's Boy and the Cat," about a boy forced to serve a tabby cat that turns out to be a princess; "The Iron Stove," about toads that turn out to be the children of kings; and "Snow White and Rose Red," which focuses on two daughters who meet a bear that turns out to be—what else?—a handsome prince. Still others include "The Raven Prince," "King Swan," "Hurleburlebutz," "The Donkey," "The Hut in the Forest," and "Hans the Hedgehog."

Only one Grimm tale, "The Singing, Springing Lark," is

INTERFOTO/ALAMY

SNOW WHITE is shown with the Seven Dwarfs in this 1903 German lithograph. "Fairy tales usually begin when the child's life in some manner has reached an impasse," wrote Bruno Bettelheim in *The Uses of Enchantment*. "In 'Snow White,' it is not any external difficulty such as poverty but the relations between her and her parents which create the problematic situation."

STAATLICHE MUSEEN ZU BERLIN/ANDREAS KILGER/ART RESOURCE, NY

AGE FOTOSTOCK/ALAMY

a more or less literal version of "Beauty and the Beast," with the added influence of "East of the Sun, West of the Moon," a Norwegian fairy tale. But like everyone else who told and retold the story over the years, Wilhelm—the chief editor—introduced elements reflecting his own experience and sensibility. In his version, the Beast is a lion, and the unnamed Beauty character asks for a lark rather than a rose. "The bird's song and ability to soar through the air are emblematic of the heroine's spunk and spirit," wrote Maria Tatar in *The Annotated Brothers Grimm.* "Like the rose, which has iconic significance as a symbol of beauty... the bird is emblematic of the heroine's character."

Wilhelm's Christianity also influenced the work. "Despite the fact that the tale relies on magic, the Grimms included several religious allusions, with one at the end of the story referring to God's lifting of the spell,"

CONTINUED ON PAGE 37

AN OIL ON CANVAS portrait, circa 1855, of the brothers Jacob and Wilhelm Grimm, above. Opposite: An alley with traditional houses on the *Deutsche Märchenstrasse* (German Fairy Tale Route) in Hesse, Germany—part of a 370-mile thoroughfare that leads from Hanau to Bremen, passing sights that inspired German fairy tales.

BPK BILDAGENTUR/ART RESOURCE, NY

MARY EVANS

THE WITCH TRIES to fatten Hansel in this 1880 lithograph, above. "The child's striving to hold on to his parents even though the time has come for meeting the world on his own is stressed," according to fairy tale theorist Bruno Bettelheim, "as well as the need to transcend a primitive orality, symbolized by the children's infatuation with the gingerbread house." At right: In this 1905 illustration for the Grimms' "The Story of the Youth Who Went Forth to Learn What Fear Was," a boy beats a fierce old man. The story has never had a major film adaptation, though Muppets master Jim Henson used it for "Fearnot," an episode of his late-1980s series, *The Storyteller.*

TOPICAL PRESS AGENCY/GETTY

MARY EVANS

THE "INNOCENCE" of childhood is a relatively modern concept, and many fairy tales reflect the ordeals that children were, once upon a time, routinely subjected to. In the 1901 photo opposite, boys are shown cleaning coal in a pit in Bargoed, Wales. Above: Tom the Piper's Son is pummeled for stealing a pig in this 1884 illustration of the popular British nursery rhyme. It is part of the Mother Goose collection of tales and poems that was among the first purely entertaining—rather than instructive—literature written for children.

CONTINUED FROM PAGE 32

Tatar added. "The overlay of piety seems out of place in a narrative about dragons, cosmic helpers, and dresses that shine like the sun."

Like the racy French and Italian versions of "Beauty and the Beast," the Grimms' early tales were clearly not for children—despite their first volume's title. Initially published in 1812, the brothers' *Kinder- und Hausmärchen* (*Tales of Children and Homes*) featured incestuous fathers, murdering mommies, mutilation, cannibalism, and other unpleasantness. In "The Robber Bridegroom," for instance, a girl is forced to drink wine until her heart bursts; she's then stripped and eviscerated. The stepsisters in "Cinderella" are so desperate to fit into the glass slipper that they cut off their toes; later, birds peck out their eyes. In "The Juniper Tree," a woman kills her son and cooks him into a stew, which she serves to her husband, who promptly asks for seconds. And forget kissing frogs to find princes: In "The Frog King," a story that bears a considerable resemblance to "Beauty and the Beast," the young heroine simply throws her amorous amphibian against the wall.

Take *that,* Walt Disney.

"To my knowledge, they never

CONTINUED ON PAGE 40

H & D ZIELSKE / LOOK-FOTO/GETTY

UNIVERSAL HISTORY ARCHIVE/UIG/GETTY

AN ANCIENT German forest—or *Wald*—in Hesse, Germany, looking much as it would have in the Grimms' time, at left. Above: "At last she met the bridegroom who was coming slowly back," Arthur Rackham's illustration for "Fitcher's Bird" in a late-19th-century edition of the Grimms' tales.

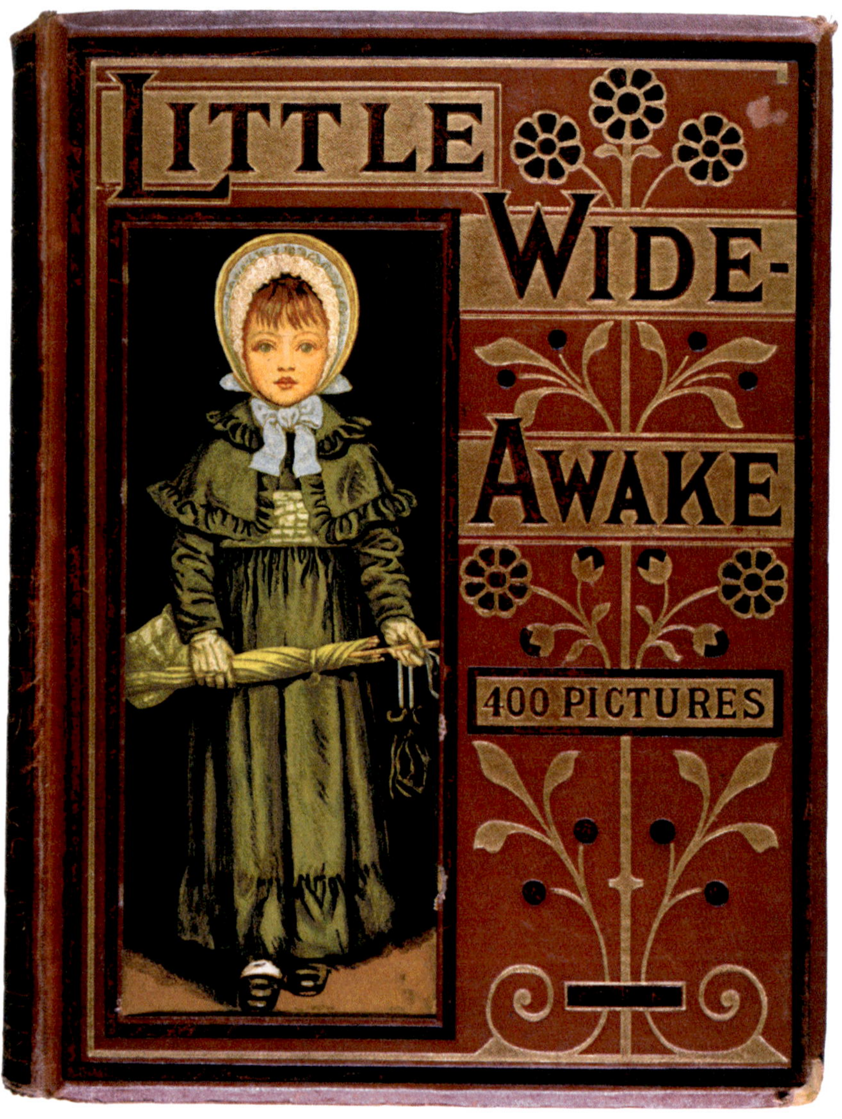

MARY EVANS

CONTINUED FROM PAGE 37

explicitly explained why they chose *Tales of Children and Homes* as a title," Jack Zipes tells LIFE. "They had footnotes, prefaces, and postscripts in all seven editions of their large collection that indicate their books were addressed to scholars and adults."

But the brothers altered this approach after children's literature itself began to change in the 1740s. "The books that were published especially for children before the mid 18th century were almost always remorselessly instructional (spelling books, school books, conduct books) or deeply pious," according to M.O. Grenby, professor of 18th-century studies in the school of English at Newcastle University.

In 1744, Englishman John Newbery successfully published *A Little Pretty Pocket-Book Intended for the Instruction and Amusement of Little Master Tommy and Pretty Miss Polly,* proving that children's books could sell. (The Newbery Medal, which annually honors the best American children's book, was named in his honor.) The popularity of these books was not lost on the penurious Grimms, whose first edition of their tales had failed to attract an audience.

In 1819, Wilhelm began removing the stories' most violent and sexual elements to reflect the child-friendly attitudes and mores of 19th-century Christian Germany. The Rapunzel who had clearly had premarital sex with the prince in the Grimms' earliest published story, for instance, chastely married him in the revisions. Incestuous

CONTINUED ON PAGE 44

JOHN MACLELLAN/MARY EVANS

LITTLE WIDE-AWAKE, an 1880 poetry book for children, at left. Opposite: A girl and a large mouse read a book under a tree in this children's book illustration from 1905. The transformation of children's books from programmatic tracts to larky literature began in the late 1700s with the publisher and bookseller John Newbery, who proved that nonutilitarian books for kids could sell.

ADVENTURES
OF
HIS MAJESTY
PUG
PETER

TOM GILLMOR/MARY EVANS

TAIS POLICANTI/GETTY

"O RAPUNZEL, Rapunzel! Let down thine hair," cries the Prince in this 1880 illustration, above. The original Rapunzel story involved premarital sex and pregnancy—elements that the Grimms later removed to make the stories kid-friendly. At right: An aqueduct in Wilhelmshöhe Park in Hesse, Germany, the area where the Brothers Grimm lived for most of their lives.

THALIASTOCK/MARY EVANS

KHARBINE-TAPABOR/REX/SHUTTERSTOCK

CONTINUED FROM PAGE 40

fathers became demons; murderous mommies became evil stepmothers; and heroines kissed—rather than tossed—royal frogs.

Wilhelm also emphasized the tales' Teutonic aspects, including the importance of the oak-filled *Wald* (forest) as a symbol of German identity. And he was influenced by the prevailing philosophical movement of the time, German Romanticism, which emphasized the irrational, the rustic, and the supernatural—as opposed to the French focus on courtliness and urbanity.

Since the Grimms had largely gathered their stories from locals, they claimed that their material was "purely German in its origins." But this ignored or otherwise obscured the fact that, like all fairy tales, the stories had international—and intertwined—roots, with Oriental, Italian, Scandinavian, and Slavic sources, according to Zipes. The most famous of them had come from—*mein Gott!*—the literature of Germany's enemy France, where the modern version of "Beauty and the Beast" had originated. (Think "Little Red Riding Hood," "Snow White," and "Sleeping Beauty.")

The oral source of these particular

SLEEPING BEAUTY in an 1885 engraving, above. At right: The Prince discovers Snow White in her coffin in a 1905 Munich fairy tale calendar. Both these heroines fought female villains before being rescued by men. "Figures of female evil stride through the best-loved, classic fairy tales," wrote Marina Warner in *From the Beast to the Blonde*: "on this earth, wicked stepmothers, ugly sisters; from fairyland, bad fairies, witches, ogresses."

BLANCHE-NEIGE

tales is identified in the Grimms' footnotes only as "Marie." Though Wilhelm's oldest son, Herman, long claimed that Marie had been his father-in-law's housekeeper, she was in fact a friend from a bourgeois French-speaking family. "Her nursemaids naturally told French stories," according to Wolfgang Hassenpflug, the great-great-grandson of Charlotte Grimm, the brothers' only sister. "The Grimms may at first have thought Marie's tales all came from Hesse, but the famous ones we now know came from France and the book by Charles Perrault." (Including, of course, "Beauty and the Beast.")

The Grimms had their reasons for insisting that their stories were verifiably German, but as we've seen there's no such thing as a definitive source for these tales. (The novelist Angela Carter once said that asking where a fairy tale came from is like asking who invented the meatball.) What matters is the way in which these ancient stories are transformed through each teller's sensibility and style. The Grimms had an abundance of both and kept rewriting their own versions over seven editions. Here, for instance, is the beginning of the 1812 version of their animal bridegroom story "The Frog King," translated by D.L. Ashliman:

BRITISH LIBRARY BOARD/ROBANA/ART RESOURCE, NY

PETER & DAWN COPE COLLECTION/MARY EVANS

GUSTAVE DORÉ'S 1910 image of Little Red Riding Hood, top, emphasizes the tale's latent eroticism. At left: In the Grimms' "The Wolf and the Seven Kids," a mother goat cuts open a sleeping wolf's stomach to rescue her kids, in this 1910 illustration. Opposite: "She went away accompanied by the lions," an illustration for "The Lady and the Lion" by Arthur Rackham in *The Fairy Tales of the Brothers Grimm*.

SEAN GALLUP/GETTY

EVERETT

"Once upon a time there was a princess who went out into a forest and sat next to a cool well."

Now compare this to the infinitely richer beginning of the same story, also translated by Ashliman, from the Grimms' 1857—and final—edition:

"In olden times, when wishing still did some good, there lived a king whose daughters were all beautiful, but the youngest was so beautiful that the sun itself, who, indeed, had seen so much, marveled every time it shone upon her face. In the vicinity of the king's castle there was a large, dark forest, and in this forest, beneath an old linden tree, there was a well. In the heat of the day the princess would go out into the forest and sit on the edge of the cool well."

By the time the brothers published this story, their three volumes included 210 tales with notes. They

BUILT BY THE openly gay Bavarian king Ludwig II, also known as Mad King Ludwig and the Fairy Tale King, Schloss Neuschwanstein (at left), located near Hohenschwangau, Germany, was allegedly the inspiration for Sleeping Beauty's castle at Disneyland, above.

did not live to see the founding of the German nation in 1871—Wilhelm died in 1859, with Jacob following in 1863, having just concluded defining the word *Frucht* ("fruit") in their unfinished dictionary. (It was later completed by others.) Certainly they wouldn't have anticipated that the nationalism they helped propagate would reach its deadly nadir under Adolf Hitler. His Third Reich minister of propaganda, Joseph Goebbels, warned that children could see through propaganda faster than adults, though one Nazi film producer claimed that "every fairy tale is politically alignable without raping the poetry within."

LINDA HAMILTON as the lawyer version of Beauty and Ron Perlman as her Beast in the hit show that ran on CBS from 1987 to 1990, top. Above: An episode of *Once Upon a Time*, an ABC show that uses fairy tales as inspiration for its twisty plots. At right: Angelina Jolie as the title character in *Maleficent*, a 2014 live-action film based on the witch in Disney's *Sleeping Beauty*.

EVERETT

JACK ROWAND/ABC/GETTY

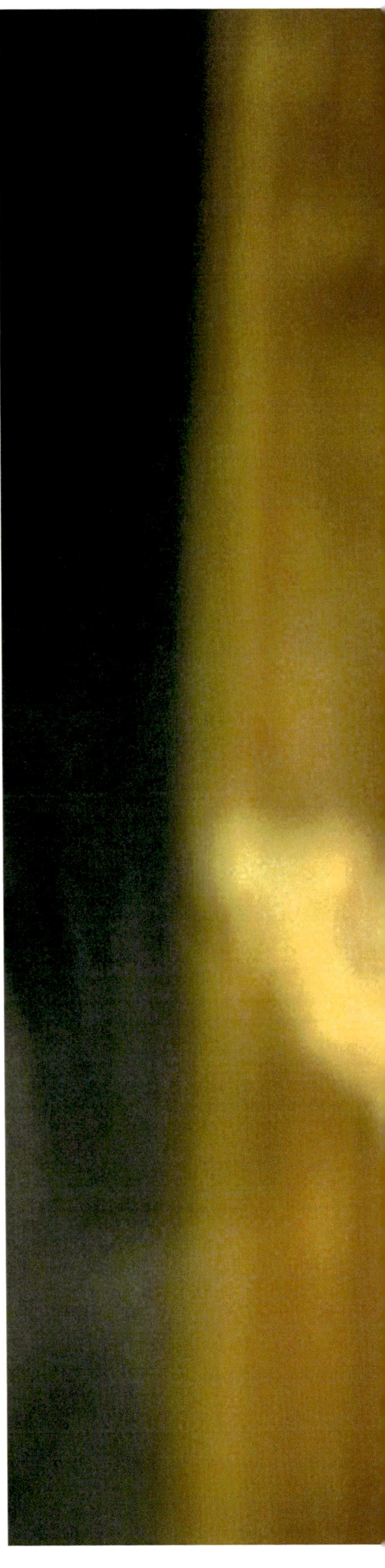

The Dark Side

"Beauty and the Beast" stays untainted as fairy tales are adapted by sinister forces

"Heil Puss in Boots! He is our Savior! We will live again!" a crowd shouts in a deliberate reflection of the Nuremberg rallies in the Nazi's cinematic version of "Puss in Boots," with Puss standing in for Hitler. Released the month after Germany invaded Poland, the Third Reich's "Little Red Riding Hood" movie featured a heroine whose cloak was emblazoned with a swastika.

Like the Grimms, the Nazis harked back to a mythic *Volk*, or people, emphasizing an "authentic" Germany untainted by "inferior" influences. In the process, they celebrated the same symbolic *Wald* that was key to the Grimms' tales—along with the anti-Semitism that animated such stories as "The Jew in the Brambles," in which the title character, a thief and "dirty dog," is forced to dance in a thicket of thorns by a man playing a magic fiddle.

"The Jew's legs started moving, and he leapt into the air," the story reads. "The man kept fiddling, and the Jew kept dancing, but thorns soon tore the Jew's dirty coat, stroked his long goatee, and jabbed and stabbed his body from head to toe. 'Oh, my!' the Jew cried. 'Please stop playing! I don't want to keep dancing!' But the man played on, thinking, 'You have stolen from people many times, and now the thorns are stealing from you!'"

Not surprisingly, the Nazis did not adapt "Beauty and the Beast," since the "pure" Beauty and the "alien" Beast live happily ever after—a scenario that was antithetical to the Aryan ideal.

A 1909 ILLUSTRATION for the Grimms' anti-Semitic fairy tale "The Jew in the Brambles," revealing the often ugly underside of fairy tales that has been both leveraged and whitewashed over the centuries.

THE SHARP ILLUSTRATION COLLECTION/MARY EVANS

Rackham. 1900

EVERETT

HERBERT HOFFMANN/ULLSTEIN BILD/GRANGER

But four months after the Germans surrendered, French poet and filmmaker Jean Cocteau directed the first movie version of the Beaumont tale, creating a masterpiece that would influence both future adaptations of the story and cinema itself.

"When it comes to 'fairy-tale movies'... there is Cocteau's *Beauty and the Beast* and then there is everything else," wrote the critic Geoffrey O'Brien. "It is a safe bet that no one who surrenders to it at an impressionable age ever quite escapes the distinct and disturbing enchantments it sets in motion."

Cocteau himself said that he wanted to make "a film that would plunge me into a lustral bath of childhood"—and indeed it succeeds in doing so for all viewers—but given the deprivations of war-ravaged France, it's a miracle that *La Belle et la Bête* was ever made at all. "Old cameras jammed, old lenses developed flaws, no two batches of film were alike, electric current failed or was bureaucratically cut off," wrote Cocteau's biographer Francis Steegmuller. "There was small choice of fabrics for costumes; sheets without patches were sought everywhere for the farmyard laundry scene; the curtains of Beauty's bed were stolen from the set."

Cocteau was vexed. ("What a pity France cannot afford the luxury of color films," he wrote in his diary.) But the limitations arguably helped the film, which would now be

HITLER YOUTH (above) reading Nazi-approved literature. The fairy tales of the Grimms and Charles Perrault were used by the Nazis as propaganda for children. A purer vision: Josette Day as Belle and Jean Marais as the Beast in Jean Cocteau's 1946 film (opposite).

SUNSET BOULEVARD/CORBIS/GETTY

unimaginable in color. Even Cocteau admitted that Henri Alekan's cinematography was like "a piece of old silver which has been polished until it shines like new... Alekan knows in advance the strangeness I'm after."

"Children believe in stories they are told," reads the film's dedication. "They have complete faith. They believe a plucked rose may bring tragic consequences to a family. They believe in the smoking hands of a man-beast who kills in the shame he feels before the maiden who is his guest. They believe in countless other artless things. It is a little of that artlessness that I ask of you. So that the omens may smile upon all, let me pronounce those four magic words, that veritable open sesame of childhood: 'Once upon a time.'"

Harking back to Gianfrancesco Straparola's emphasis on animal magnetism, the bland prince who emerges at the end of Cocteau's film seems far less appealing than his bestial predecessor. "Even as Belle and her prince... soar into the sky, she seems already to realize that this is not exactly what she wanted," wrote O'Brien. (At one screening of the film, Greta Garbo reportedly exclaimed, "Give me back my Beast!")

So another psychological wrinkle was added to the story—implicitly, at least—which helped to fuel the psychoanalytic and academic analysis of fairy tales that followed. The chief figure in this trend was

MARAIS AS THE BEAST and Day as Belle in Cocteau's classic film. "One must have Marais's passion for his work and his devotion to his dog, to persevere as he did in deserting the human race for the animal race," Cocteau wrote.

DILTZ/BRIDGEMAN IMAGES

SUNSET BOULEVARD/CORBIS/GETTY

"IT TOOK ME five hours to make up," said Marais of playing the Beast, at left with Day. "That meant 13 hours a day in the studio. Because of the fangs attached to my teeth, all I could eat was mush, and that by the spoonful." Above: Marais (standing), Cocteau (in white sweater), and an unidentified man on the film's set.

Bruno Bettelheim, a Holocaust survivor and professor of psychology at the University of Chicago. In his groundbreaking 1976 book, *The Uses of Enchantment,* he claimed that "Beauty and the Beast" was about "the humanization and socialization of the id by the superego."

In layman's terms, this means that our wildest impulses can be domesticated by civilization and self-control. "The highest psychic qualities (Psyche) are to be wedded to sexuality (Eros)," wrote Bettelheim. "Spiritual man must be reborn to become ready for the marriage of sexuality with wisdom." More specifically, Bettelheim suggested that the tale reflects a female "evolution from immaturity to maturity."

"No other well-known fairy tale makes it as obvious as 'Beauty and the Beast' that a child's oedipal attachment to a parent is natural, desirable, and has the most positive consequences of all, if during the process of maturation it is transferred and transformed as it becomes detached from the parent and concentrated on the lover," he wrote.

But academics have never entirely succeeded in pigeonholing fairy tales. "Their failure is predictable because the genre is so volatile and fluid," Jack Zipes says. The stories also resist any effort to align them with historical

CONTINUED ON PAGE 62

ANDRÉ PAULVÉ
PRÉSENTE
UN FILM DE
Jean Cocteau
JEAN MARAIS
JOSETTE DAY
dans
la BELLE
HISTOIRE, PAROLES, MISE EN SCÈNE DE JEAN COCTEAU
CHRISTIA
avec
MILA PARELY, NANE GERMON, MI
CONSEILLER TECHNIQUE: R.CLÉMENT IMAGES DE ALEKAN MUSIC
UNE SUPERPRODUC

A POSTER for the film that Cocteau described as a plunge into "a lustral bath of childhood." Of film directing, he wrote: "There is nothing more glorious than to write a poem with people, faces, hands, lights, objects, arranging them all as one likes."

EVERETT

SCALA/ART RESOURCE, NY

BPK BILDAGENTUR/ART RESOURCE, NY

CONTINUED FROM PAGE 59

fact. In addition to Petrus Gonsalvus, for instance, many real-life figures have been cited as inspirations for the tales.

"Bluebeard" is said to have been based on the 15th-century child killer Gilles de Rais, a friend of Joan of Arc's and a hero of the Hundred Years' War. Some suggest that Snow White was modeled on the 16th-century German noblewoman Margarete von Waldeck, whose brother is said to have owned a copper mine where brutal conditions stunted the child workers, causing them to be called "dwarfs."

"Rapunzel" may have been based on the legend of Saint Barbara, who refused to renounce her Christian faith even as the Romans forced her father to cut off her head. (He was supposedly struck and killed by lightning shortly afterward.) And "Hansel and Gretel" might reflect the great European famine of 1315–1317.

Of course these theories are intriguing, but they're ultimately beside the point, if not pointless. "The only reason to historicize these stories is to understand their origins and the contexts in which they were told," says Maria Tatar. "They are archetypes that are culturally inflected in

GRAIN IS DISTRIBUTED **outside of Orsanmichele, a church in Florence, Italy, after the 1315 famine, at left. In the midst of this crisis, children were sometimes abandoned by their parents—a fact reflected in such tales as "Hansel and Gretel," shown in an 1880 lithograph, opposite.**

ARCHIVIO GBB/CONTRASTO/REDUX

different times and places."

Crucially the gap between the ancient oral traditions and our modern focus on individual authors and their books was most notably bridged by a Danish shoemaker's son—a gangly, awkward genius whose work was often fueled by unrequited love.

"GIVE ME A LIVELIHOOD! GIVE ME a bride! My blood wants love, as my heart does!" Hans Christian Andersen wrote in his diary.

Born into poverty in Odense, Denmark, in 1805, the author of such classic fairy tales as "The Little Mermaid" and "The Ugly Duckling" spent his life as a wealthy, well-traveled, famous writer who was nevertheless always in the throes of thwarted romance. Painful as it was, Andersen's raw, often childlike emotion inspired him to bring a more human dimension to the genre—specifically to the awkward interspecies love reflected by the animal bridegroom tales.

Like the Beast, Andersen saw himself as an alien desperately in love with unattainable humans. The first object of his hopeless affection was Riborg Voigt, the love of his twenties. "Oh, she is so beautiful, so gentle, and good, you would love her, so would all the world," he wrote to a friend. Other fixations included Sophie Orsted, the 16-year-old daughter of a famous physicist, as well as any number of

HANS CHRISTIAN ANDERSEN is shown in an 1879 portrait at the window of his house, at left. Above: An 1890 view of the entrance to Tivoli Gardens, in Copenhagen, which first opened in 1843. The park's pagodas, lanterns, and assorted chinoiserie helped inspire Andersen's "The Nightingale," which he called "the Chinese tale."

ULLSTEIN BILD/GETTY

CULTURE CLUB/GETTY

On the morrow the wild ducks saw him. "And who may you be?" said they; "you certainly are an ugly fellow, but we don't mind that so long as you don't want to marry into our family." Poor ugly duckling! he was only too happy to be allowed to eat and drink and sleep in the rushes.

BRITISH LIBRARY BOARD/ROBANA/ART RESOURCE, NY

young men—including a duke, a Danish dancer, and Voigt's brother.

These frustrated amorous attachments deeply influenced Andersen's work—in fact, they were inseparable from it. ("The history of my life will be the best commentary on my work," he oncc wrotc.) The greatest of his stories—"The Little Match Girl," "The Steadfast Tin Soldier," "The Fir Tree," among others—are about suffering outsiders; as such, they are often astonishingly dark. "From 'The Little Mermaid' (1836) onward, his tales, comically or tragically, are the story of himself as failed lover and struggling artist," wrote Jackie Wullschlager in an introduction to the tales.

The story of a mermaid who is willing to sacrifice her life and identity to gain a human soul (just as the Beast seeks to regain his), "The Little Mermaid" was inspired by the bisexual Andersen's unrequited love for his friend Edvard Collin. "He had spent years trying to express the feelings he was not allowed to speak

CONTINUED ON PAGE 71

AN ILLUSTRATION by Theo Van Hoytema for Andersen's "The Ugly Duckling," above. Opposite: An illustration from the 1800s for "The Little Mermaid," the first tale to reflect Andersen's lifelong experience of unrequited love. "I don't know how other writers feel!" he wrote. "I suffer with my characters, I share their moods, whether good or bad."

SISSIE BRIMBERG/NATIONAL GEOGRAPHIC/GETTY

EDVARD ERIKSEN'S sculpture of the Little Mermaid has watched over Copenhagen's harbor since 1913. Through the years, she has been beheaded, dismembered, blown up, covered with paint, and sent to China for Shanghai's Expo 2010.

YADID LEVY/ANZENBERGER/REDUX

DEAGOSTINI/GETTY

A 1916 ILLUSTRATION for Andersen's "The Nightingale" by Harry Clarke, at left. Above: The pagoda in Tivoli Gardens that helped inspire the tale, along with Andersen's typically unrequited crush on the opera singer Jenny Lind, the so-called Swedish Nightingale.

CONTINUED FROM PAGE 66

out," Wullschlager wrote, "and he empathized with his mermaid—in her sense of being a different species than humankind." (Another of his unrequited loves was the Swedish opera singer Jenny Lind, known as the Swedish Nightingale, who—along with a visit to Tivoli Gardens—inspired his classic tale "The Nightingale.")

Though Andersen became the most famous writer in Europe, mirroring the transformation of his Ugly Duckling, he remained an unhappy, depressive, and loveless man. When he died in 1875, an old letter from Riborg Voigt was found in a purse around his neck. He had not become a handsome prince—nor did he ever meet his Beauty.

He certainly didn't live happily ever after.

Unlike the Grimms, Andersen did not adapt folktales but "drew on traditional oral narratives to create his own literary narratives that, in turn, became—like 'The Little Mermaid'—folklore, migrating into new media," says Tatar. In the process, he brought a interior dimension to the tradition. "He gives us characters with an inner life—we suffer with them, something you rarely find in fairy tales, which externalize all emotions.

If someone is unhappy, they burst into tears."

This was just one of many innovations that would help bring the fairy tale into the 20th and 21st centuries. "The fairy tale continues to grow and to embrace, if not swallow, all types of genres, art forms, and cultural institutions," says Zipes. "It adjusts itself to new environments through the human disposition to re-create relevant narratives and through technologies that make its diffusion easier and more effective—painting, photography, radio, film, and so on."

Indeed, the new media of the 20th century led to further iterations of "Beauty and the Beast"—including an opera by Philip Glass (written to accompany the Cocteau film), a hit CBS TV series featuring the Beauty as a lawyer—and, most notably, an animated feature produced by a movie studio on the brink of bankruptcy.

THE PHILIP GLASS ENSEMBLE, with baritone Gregory Purnhagen (left) and mezzo soprano Hai-Ting Chinn (right), performed Glass's operatic score for *La Belle et la Bête* live with the film in Santa Barbara, California, in 2014. (The original score for the film is by French composer Georges Auric.)

BELLE AND HER animalistic amour begin to fall in love in the 1991 Disney classic *Beauty and the Beast,* which successfully updated the ancient tale for modern audiences.

The Disney Versions

Beauty and the Beast reanimates the studio that defined the modern fairy tale

Once upon a time—in the 1920s, to be exact—a young animator named Walt Disney met a stranger on a train who was interested in the fact that he produced motion pictures. But "when Disney told him that he made cartoons, the man lost interest," Stephen Cavalier, author of *The World History of Animation* and owner of Spy Pictures, an animation company, tells LIFE. "This is the kind of attitude that riled Disney and drove him, for a while at least, to make something more grown-up and serious and respected."

Though the "grown-up" project the filmmaker finally tackled in the 1930s was based on a children's story, *Snow White and the Seven Dwarfs* changed motion pictures—and pop culture itself—forever, becoming the first feature-length animated film and the most successful American film up to that time. It had been called "Disney's folly," but *Time* magazine presciently called it "an authentic masterpiece, to be shown in theaters and beloved by new generations long after the current crop of Hollywood stars, writers, and directors are sleeping where no Prince's kiss can wake them."

Though Disney reportedly wanted to adapt "Beauty and the Beast" as an animated feature, the project never got off the ground. "Probably before *Cinderella,* Walt asked us to read 'Beauty and the Beast' and come up with some ideas for it," Disney animator Ollie Johnston once said. "The story guys may have done some

COLLECTION CHRISTOPHEL/ALAMY

MARY EVANS/DISNEY/RONALD GRANT/EVERETT

work on it, but I never heard anymore about it." Why? According to Frank Thomas, another of Disney's animators, that's because the tale was too restrictive and illogical for modern tastes: Why did the Beast punish Beauty's father for merely picking a rose? Why was the rose so important? How can you create compelling drama from the story of a heroine who sits in a castle, simply following her father's instructions?

So Disney moved on to other projects, helping to revive and burnish the reputation of the Brothers Grimm and Charles Perrault in the process, while perpetuating what some decried as a sanitized, whitewashed version of the tales. (No seductive fathers or murdering mommies in sight.) But after 1959's expensive *Sleeping Beauty* proved a box office disappointment, he mostly abandoned the material.

In the wake of Disney's death in 1966, his company floundered. In fact, it was on the brink of bankruptcy in the late 1980s when Jeffrey Katzenberg, then the chief of Walt Disney Studios, tried to revive the animation division. He had his work cut out for him. Disney's films were tanking at the box office, and the company hadn't produced a full-length animated fairy tale in 30 years.

©RKO RADIO PICTURES, COURTESY PHOTOFEST

WALT DISNEY CO./EVERETT (2)

CLOCKWISE FROM TOP: Walt Disney's *Snow White and the Seven Dwarfs* (1937), *Sleeping Beauty* (1959), *Cinderella* (1950), and Disney himself working on storyboards for *Sleeping Beauty*. "All Disney's powers of invention failed to save the princes from featureless banality and his heroines from saccharin sentimentality," Marina Warner wrote in *From the Beast to the Blonde*. "Authentic power lies with the bad women."

But Katzenberg had a secret weapon on the East Coast.

He was Howard Ashman, the author, lyricist, and director behind *Little Shop of Horrors,* a 1982 Off Broadway musical based on a 1960s B movie about a man-eating plant. Featuring music by Ashman's collaborator, Alan Menken, the adaptation became an unlikely hit, eventually playing on Broadway. Not long afterward, Katzenberg called Ashman from Los Angeles with a question: Did he want to work on an animated musical based on Hans Christian Andersen's "The Little Mermaid"?

"IT'S VERY DIFFICULT TO TAKE THE originals and convert them into a story that works for the '90s," said screenwriter Linda Woolverton of her attempt to find inspiration in the early versions of "Beauty and the Beast." In the late 1980s, Disney had hired her to write a script for a feature-length animated version of the tale. "You have to consider what kids are like now in terms of sophistication, you have to make sure that your themes are strong, that people can relate to the characters, that the story isn't sexist."

After *The Little Mermaid* became a hit, winning the 1989 Oscar for Best Original Score, Katzenberg asked Ashman and Menken to help

CONTINUED ON PAGE 82

PHOTOFEST

© BUENA VISTA PICTURES, COURTESY PHOTOFEST

HOWARD ASHMAN (left) reads *Little Brother and Little Sister,* a collection of fairy tales given to him by his sister, Sarah. "It would have been Christmas 1985 or 1986," she tells LIFE, "and was photographed at my apartment on West 55th Street in Manhattan." Above: *Little Shop of Horrors* (top), the hit musical Ashman wrote and directed, and *The Little Mermaid,* his first project for Disney.

BUYENLARGE/GETTY

ENTERTAINMENT PICTURES/ALAMY

EVER SINCE Jeanne-Marie Leprince de Beaumont's version of "Beauty and the Beast," a key element of the story has involved the Beast asking Beauty to marry him over dinner. Compare the illustration by Walter Crane (at top) with this scene from Disney's 1991 animated feature.

ENTERTAINMENT PICTURES/ALAMY

© DISNEY, COURTESY PHOTOFEST

LUMIERE, THE CANDELABRA; Mrs. Potts, the teapot; and Cogsworth, the clock, in Disney's 1991 animated feature (above top) were voiced by David Ogden Stiers (Cogsworth), Angela Lansbury (Mrs. Potts), and Jerry Orbach (Lumiere), shown just above. Opposite: The film's supervising animator, Glen Keane.

WALT DISNEY CO./EVERETT

CONTINUED FROM PAGE 78

Woolverton with *Beast.* Though Ashman wanted to work on *Aladdin,* which was also in development, he reluctantly agreed—and almost single-handedly revived the project. "Howard," Woolverton later said, "is really good at plot."

In the Beaumont tale, the Beast asks Beauty if she will marry him over dinner every night—and every night she says no. But if the movie had been based solely on this trope, Ashman said, it would have been about nothing more than two people having dinner. "You can do that once," said one collaborator, "but after that it's not very entertaining." Instead, Ashman brought a new twist to the story: "The Beast is the guy with the problem," he said. "He's got to redeem himself by the movie's end. His act of love allows the girl to leave his castle."

He also emphasized simplicity and emotion. "He would always make us stop going off on tangents and come back to the purity of the source, the emotion of the source," Woolverton said. "Howard told us that every single scene . . . should have an umbrella of emotion over it, whether it's

CONTINUED ON PAGE 86

WALT DISNEY CO./EVERETT

BEAUTY AND THE BEAST waltz in the 1991 animated feature. "The dance, for me, is really where the audience starts to see it happening and starts knowing that it is happening," Emma Watson, who plays Belle in the live-action remake, told *Entertainment Weekly*. "This is total, blissful escapism."

COLLECTION CHRISTOPHEL/ALAMY

CONTINUED FROM PAGE 82

warmth or terror or love or drama or even comedy. Every single scene."

Ashman had the golden touch, but he was obviously in poor health. He claimed that "his weight loss was due to colitis or a hernia," Menken later said. "And we all happily believed him." But after their Oscar win for *The Little Mermaid,* Ashman told Menken that he was HIV positive. He did not have long to live.

On March 10, 1991, the first screening of *Beauty and the Beast* was greeted with rapturous acclaim. Though Ashman was too sick to attend, the creative team visited him in the hospital afterward, asking, "Who would have thought it would turn out this great?"

"I would've," Ashman said.

Four days later, he died.

The third highest grossing film of 1991, *Beauty and the Beast* became the first animated feature to be nominated for a Best Picture Oscar and later became a hit Broadway musical that ran for 13 years. The film was dedicated to "our friend Howard, who gave a mermaid her voice and a beast his soul. We will be forever grateful."

"I CAN'T EVEN THINK HOW MANY times I watched it as a child," the actress Emma Watson recently told *Entertainment Weekly.* She plays Belle in the live-action version of the animated classic, slated for release on March 17. "I knew all the words by heart. I knew all the songs by heart."

CONTINUED ON PAGE 90

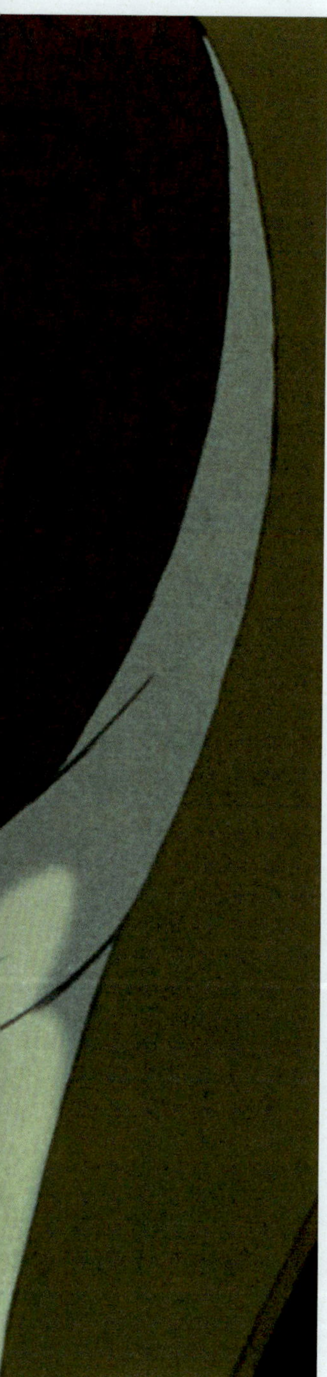

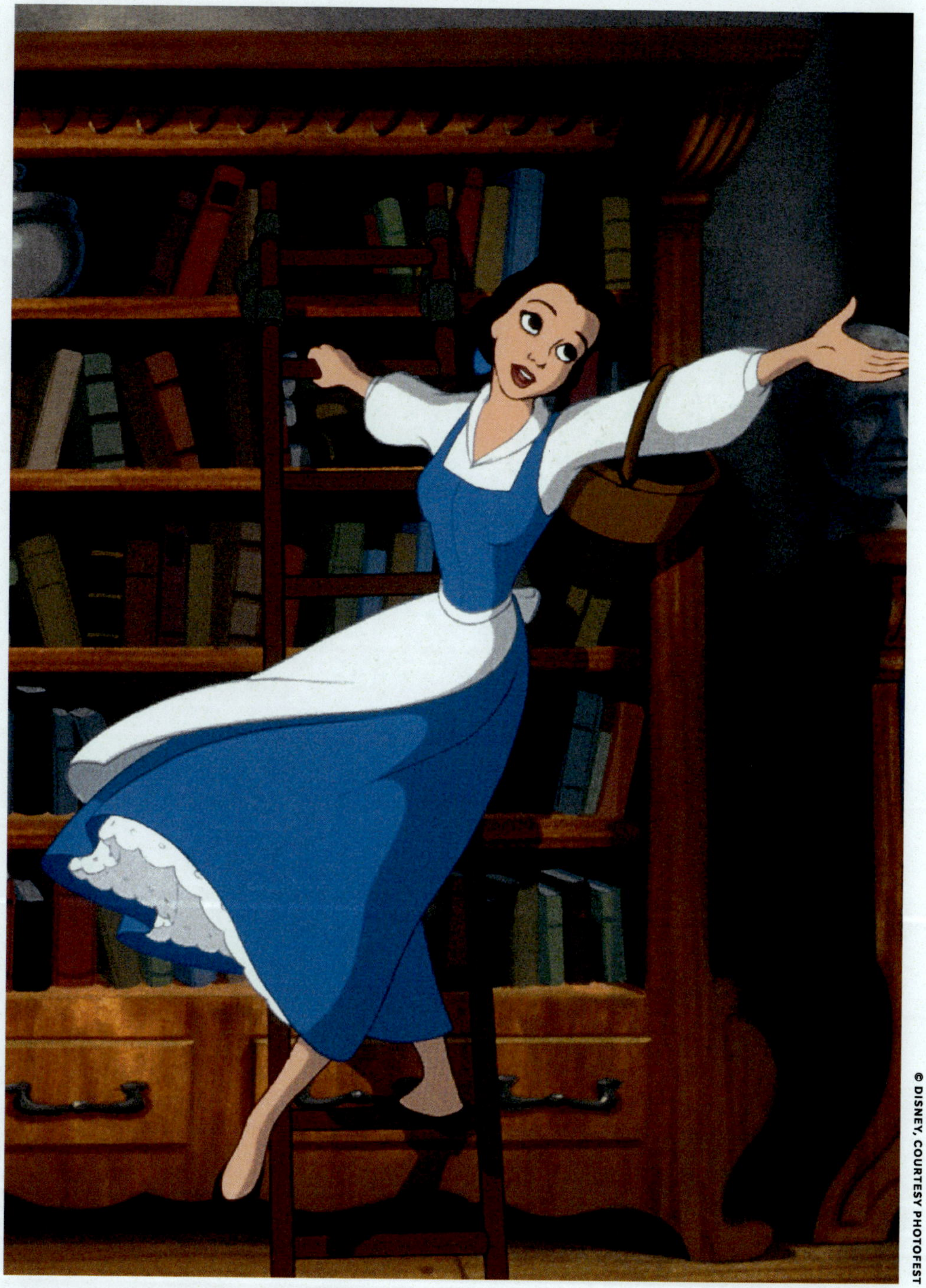

© DISNEY, COURTESY PHOTOFEST

THE BEAST is shown with the enchanted rose, at left: If he can learn to love before the last petal falls, the spell that turned him into a beast will be broken. Above: "I think Belle as a character represents a woman who is willing to stand outside of what is expected of her," Watson told *EW*.

LUKE EVANS as Gaston in the live-action remake. Lost lyrics were added to the song "Gaston," Evans told *EW*. "So, for the [audience members] who know the songs immensely well, which I think is most people, you will hear a few new lines, which are really, really special."

MOVIESTORE/REX/SHUTTERSTOCK

CONTINUED FROM PAGE 86

Costarring Dan Stevens (*Downton Abbey*) as the Beast, the new film also offers new songs by Menken and Andrew Lloyd Webber's frequent lyricist Tim Rice. There are previously unheard lyrics from Ashman, too. "We had a treasure trove of lyrics that Howard had written that we did not put in the movie," Menken told *EW*. "When Bill Condon [the director] found out about those lyrics, he said, 'Oh my god, can we please look at that, because it would be a wonderful way to add an extra freshness to the movie.' So, yes, you're going to hear some unheard Howard Ashman lyrics."

They are, however, "a little bit risqué," Menken said. Shades of "The Pig King"? Not exactly. "Not risqué sexually," Menken said. "But risqué in terms of sensibility. We all felt ready to have these lyrics."

Much has changed since 1991, of course—both culturally and technologically. Computer animation has replaced traditional cel-based work, and CGI has become the go-to technology for special effects. As a result, Stevens "basically has to perform his role twice," said *EW*'s Clark Collis. "He does a neck-down performance and then a neck-up performance. Now the neck-down performance—he's on these practical sets interacting with Emma Watson. He's on stilts because the Beast is really tall. He's in a motion-capture suit, and he's sort of acting out the below-neck performance for the Beast. Then . . . he goes into a studio, where his face is covered in some sort of ultraviolet paint. And then he does the neck-up

MOVIESTORE/REX/SHUTTERSTOCK

IN THE ANIMATED version of the tale, Belle's father, Maurice, is an inventor. In this year's live-action remake, Belle herself is the inventor. Here Belle (Watson) is shown with Maurice (Kevin Kline) and the music boxes he constructs.

performance as the Beast in front of two dozen cameras that are mapping his entire face. And then those two... performances... are put into a computer... and eventually you get the performance of the Beast."

It took six months to prepare the live-action version of the animated film's iconic "Be Our Guest" number, in which the household servants—a teapot and candelabra among them—sing and dance. The scene took *another* three months to shoot—and "they're probably still tinkering with special effects six months on," Collis said. "[Condon] said that one scene cost more than all of his previous films."

Plot elements have changed, too. "We tried to tweak things to make [Belle] more proactive, and a bit less carried along by the story and a bit more in charge of—and in control of—her own destiny," Watson told *EW.*

In the animated film, for instance, Belle's father is an inventor. "We actually co-opted that for Belle," Watson said. "I was like, 'Well, there was never very much information or detail at the beginning of the story as to why Belle didn't fit in, other than she liked books. Also what is she doing with her time?' So, we created a backstory for her, which was that she had invented a kind of washing machine, so that, instead of doing laundry, she could sit and use that time to read instead. So, yeah, we made Belle an inventor."

"I REALLY EMBRACED working on the dress, making sure that it was utterly whimsical, and magical," Watson told *EW* of the live-action version of the iconic garment from the animated film. "The scene that I wear that dress in... really tells the story of Beast and Belle falling in love."

MOVIESTORE/REX/SHUTTERSTOCK

THE NEVER-ENDING STORY

Today, the prerevolutionary France where "Beauty and the Beast" originated might as well have existed once upon a time, and the villages and forests of the nationalistic Germany that fueled the Brothers Grimms' transformation of the tale have been all but replaced by high rises and highways. But a taste of the old world—and the story—can still be had along Germany's 370-mile Fairy Tale Route (*Deutsche Märchenstrasse*), which leads from Hanau to Bremen, passing castles and gardens where even now an unsuspecting merchant might unwittingly compromise his daughter by picking a rose or two.

Along the way, you can visit Grimmwelt (Grimm World) Kassel, a museum showing copies of the Grimms' stories in books inscribed with their handwritten notes and corrections.

The Grimms didn't write the most iconic version of "Beauty and the Beast," but their work helped popularize fairy tales in general, fueling the rise of Walt Disney's billion-dollar empire and its storied succession of princesses. All this recognition would no doubt have come as a surprise to the poor Hessian academics who'd begun compiling fairy tales as a favor to a friend.

Or *would* it have?

Maybe in the end the brothers knew exactly what they had accomplished: The last story in their final edition of the tales, "The Golden Key," is the only one in their oeuvre without a proper ending. Why? Perhaps its very inconclusiveness was the Grimms' way of showing us how fairy tales—"Beauty and the Beast" foremost among them—keep evolving... and therefore never really end:

THE GOLDEN KEY

By the Brothers Grimm

Once upon a wintertime, a poor boy was dragging his sled through the deep snow, collecting firewood. After he had gathered it, he was too cold to go straight home, so he built a fire to warm himself instead. As he cleared a space in the snow, he discovered a small golden key, which meant that there must also be a lock somewhere. So he dug deeper in the snow, finally unearthing a small iron chest. "There must be treasure inside!" he thought. "I hope the key fits!" The keyhole was so small, he could hardly see it at first, but thankfully the key fit. He turned it once—and now we have to wait until he finishes unlocking the box and opens the lid before we can discover what wonderful things were inside.

NO, IT'S NOT MADE of gingerbread, but this house in the Bavarian village of Oberammergau is painted with images from "Hansel and Gretel."

JUST ONE MORE

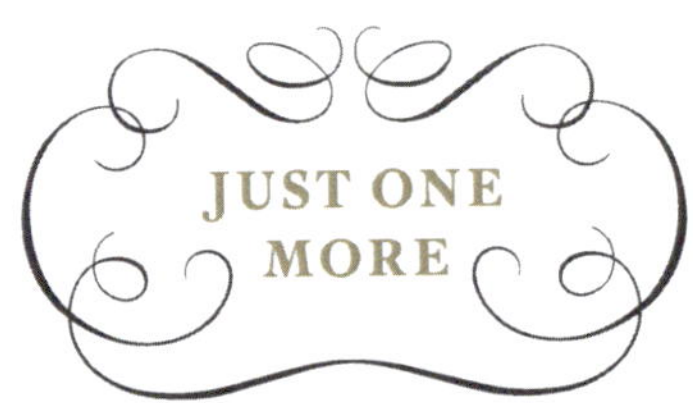

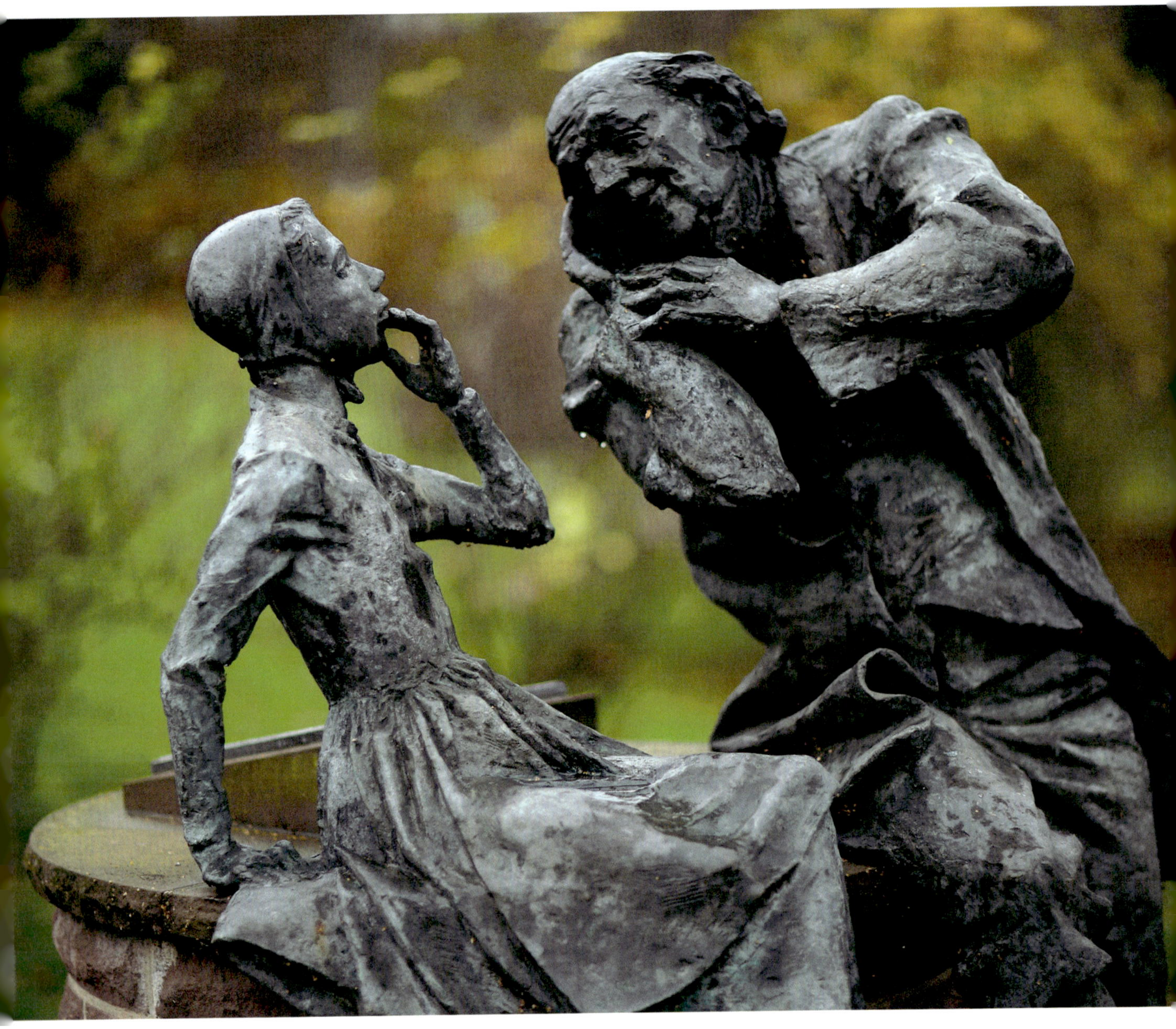

A SCULPTURE in Schöneberg, Germany, along the *Deutsche Märchenstrasse*, depicts a man telling a fairy tale to his granddaughter. Could it be "Beauty and the Beast"? *"Once upon a time, a merchant who had lost his fortune traveled overseas in search of new opportunities . . ."*

SEAN GALLUP/GETTY

Made in the USA
San Bernardino, CA
03 March 2017